FROM INDIANAPOLIS
TO LE MANS

Originally published in Italian under the title
Da Monza a Indianapolis
Copyright © 1972 by Arnoldo Mondadori Editore, Milan
English Translation copyright © 1974 by Hamlyn Publishing Group LTD
All Rights reserved
First Published in America by
Derbi Books Inc.

ISBN 0 89009 005 i c s

Library of Congress Catalogue Card Number 74-80971
Printed and Bound in Italy by Arnoldo Mondadori Editore, Verona

TOMMASO TOMMASI

FROM INDIANAPOLIS TO LE MANS

derbibooks inc.

Foreword by Juan Manuel Fangio

I consider that it was a brilliant idea to publish an illustrated book on the great racing circuits of the world, since tracks have often been left in the shade while all attention was focused on the racing drivers and their machines. Yet in my years as a racing driver, I had occasion to pass every point on the big circuits hundreds of times and I could tell a fascinating story about each curve.

Every one of us has his likes and dislikes: it is an innate thing, often tied to a pleasant or unpleasant episode. I have always enjoyed the fast circuits in particular, and I especially recall Monza; for me, a win at Monza was always like winning twice over. I was truly sorry to hear that they want to close the Monza track down. For those who are far from Italy, it is impossible to think that Monza may no longer exist; perhaps only when it's gone will everyone realize how important it was for car racing.

Another racing track which I remember with pleasure is the Nürburgring, where the skill of the driver can overcome the technical shortcomings of his car. In 1957 I won a Grand Prix there with a car which forced me to stop in the pits to change tyres; I won back the lost time by using gears higher than needed to get round the many bends on this circuit. I was able to make up for the inconvenient stop in the pits and won the race with a four second lead over my nearest rivals.

I believe in the unchanged value of car races and, even though I remember with pleasure the fascination of the long road races, I realize it is inevitable that the present trend should be taking place which requires venues suitable for driving that can be viewed; car tracks built, that is, in sites which the public can easily reach and where spectators can easily follow all the phases of a race, with tracks designed to try to the maximum the capacity of a car and the skill of its driver, guaranteeing at the same time maximum safety. In this respect it is only right that drivers should be listened to and their demands complied with since the circuits also should keep up with the evolution of car racing.

In my time we used to race without bothering overmuch about minor details: a light pair of shoes, canvas trousers, a shirt, a crash helmet and away—in search of a win. But it was the cars which, with their thinner wheels, warned you if you were over the limit; nowadays the racing cars of all formulae have huge wheels which reduce the margin of 'warning'. Times are changing and it is right to try and avoid unnecessary risks to drivers.

Going through this book, I have seen again many of the places where I raced and won, where I have been happy and sad. I think that for all racing enthusiasts it will be a pleasure to make a more thorough discovery of the great circuits where my colleagues fight their gripping duels.

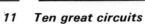

Introduction

It is virtually impossible to define the ideal motor racing circuit. There are many ways of conceiving a circuit, of offering comfort and a good view to the spectators, or of creating difficulties for the drivers. Every designer has his own way of looking at the problem and the solutions differ from one to the next, for it is right that drivers and cars should be tried on tracks of varying types: one tortuous and hilly, another very fast with long straights linked by gentle curves. Only a severe test on a circuit can show up the truly great driver and the strongest, most advanced machinery.

Our intention to offer a panorama of the world's circuits has therefore been conditioned by the need to range over all types, from the super-fast speed bowls like Indianapolis to the urban circuit, slow and winding, that snakes through the city streets, as at Monaco. We could not ignore Le Mans, scene of day-long duels, or Monza, with its breathless speeds, for these also represent particular types of circuits. We had to cover a wide range of characteristic elements in order to show how many solutions there are to the problem of putting man and machine to a severe test. At the same time we wanted to describe the various types of episodes that characterize a day's racing. This is how we chose the ten circuits examined in detail more closely than the others included in the last section of this book. Our choice, therefore, has had nothing to do with selecting the ten best circuits in the world: those that are included have been chosen in an attempt to present the reader with a meaningful picture of the background against which the great drivers have striven for victory.

Dusty town streets saw many great road races at the beginning of the 20th century. At Dieppe in 1907 the Grand Prix was the most important event in a programme of festivities that also included a floral parade and a feast in Venetian costume.

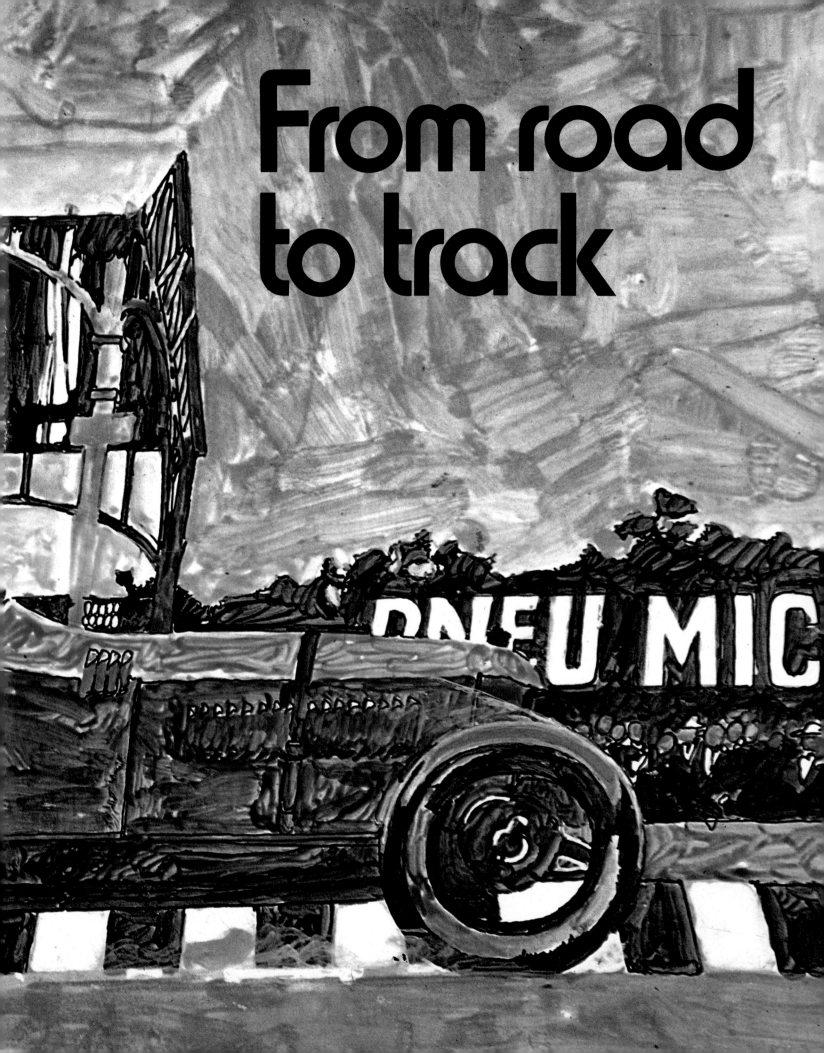

From road
to track

Automobile competition was born almost simultaneously with the motor vehicle, contributing to its rapid evolution and giving rise to some fantastic feats of motoring. The first trials, the first records and the first drivers have gone down into legend and into the annals of history.

The very early part of the story of the automobile was characterized by the 'red flag act', that is to say by the compulsory presence of a man with a red flag, who was supposed to walk in front of every motor vehicle to warn of the incipient 'danger'. It was not long before this man with his flag ended up as a cartoon figure—one obvious sign that the motor car had found its place in our everyday world, becoming an accepted part of the scenery.

It was during this pioneering period that the first competitions and the first record-breaking attempts took place. The race, since time immemorial a feature of human society, now adopted a new guise. It was no longer a matter of matching the physical strength of one man against others, but it became a way of trying out new technical developments. The first races were private affairs, but some people soon began to appreciate that contests between cars made good visual entertainment, of the type that could draw crowds.

Motor racing was first made subject to precise regulations at the beginning of the 1900s, with the Gordon Bennet Cup and the launching of the first international formula in the French Grand Prix of 1906.

Road races began to proliferate. But they inevitably brought with them the first serious accidents, and the number of these grew alarmingly as speeds increased. As a counter measure, it was believed that problems such as this could be solved by holding competitions on special courses better suited for them. Thus were born the Brooklands Motor Course, in England in 1907, and the Indianapolis Motor Speedway, in the USA, where the first 500 Miles was run in 1911. Before the First World War, therefore, a movement was already afoot to confine racing to special circuits.

Times changed rapidly, accelerated by technological progress which—

At a time when the majority of people still looked upon the car as some sort of fearful monster, races had a strong fascination. Here Felice Nazzaro's Fiat is seen passing the little church of Criel-sur-Mer in the French GP.

Work in the pits has always fascinated spectators, partly because
of the rare opportunity of seeing the cars and drivers
stationary. This picture shows the two Lorraine-Dietrichs of
Duray and Gabriel.

as always—had received a giant boost during the War. As in the case of the aeroplane, so in the case of the car the War compressed into its short span many years of technological development, and in the immediate postwar years cars began to achieve ever more exciting speeds.

There followed a revival of discussion about permanent circuits specially designed for motor racing, which would be more convenient and comfortable for the public and which—although to a comparatively limited degree—would even afford them protection against the cars.

Some of the classic road races died out, and racing began in earnest on continental Europe's first permanent circuits.

In 1922 the Monza circuit was completed and in the same year Bordino won the Italian Grand Prix in a Fiat. At Le Mans a semi-permanent circuit was prepared in 1924 for the 24 Hours. The Spa circuit, in Belgium, also came into being in 1924; and one year later at Rheims racing began on a circuit then defined as being 'for trials', which was made up of stretches of the Routes Nationales 31, 27 and 26. In Germany, the Nürburgring was completed in 1927. Two years later, the first Monaco Grand Prix was run on

the narrow streets of Monte Carlo, already famous for its casinos in which the noble and wealthy lost fortunes gambling.

From these beginnings the new style of motor racing soon established a firm place for itself in sporting history. At Monza, Nürburgring, Le Mans, Rheims and on the other circuits opened after the end of the First World War the exploits of Nuvolari, Caracciola, Varzi, Wimille, Chiron, Campari, Fagioli, Benoist, Stuck, Sommer and Ascari were breathlessly followed by the millions of spectators who flocked to see titanic duels between the champions.

As the Second World War drew near, motor racing became tainted with political undertones and then—while war raged once again—it came to a standstill, and waited for better times.

The countries that emerged victorious from the War were naturally enough the first in which motor racing was resumed. England, for instance, spawned a number of permanent circuits and Britain began to produce drivers of championship status. Thus Anglo-Saxon drivers like Moss, Collins, Hawthorn, Brooks and others found their names on the roll of honour of great racing champions alongside names like Juan Manuel Fangio and Alberto Ascari. Silverstone, Goodwood, Aintree, Oulton Park and Brands Hatch took their rightful place in motor racing history. The same was true in America, where Watkins Glen and Sebring very soon became famous enough to be mentioned in the same breath as Indianapolis, the huge arena which has seen such thrilling duels and fearful accidents.

By this time motor racing technology had reached a point at which constructors, organizers and the authorities responsible for public order regarded artificial circuits with ever greater confidence and road races with ever greater anxiety. The great tradition of the road race received the *coup de grâce* in 1957 when a Ferrari driven by the Spanish nobleman Alfonso de Portago plunged into the crowd, killing many. This spelt the end of the classic Mille Miglia and the triumph of the enemies of motor

The search for improvement and development, and the desire to excel, motivated the people in and behind the early races. The first front-wheel-drive car to participate in a European race was built by Walter J. Christie.

racing, of those who do not understand the fascination of speed and do not accept man's freedom to choose his own risks.

These were hard times for motor racing; times too for reflection for those who understood and defended the cause. After the controversy had died down, it was recognized that motor sport had a right to exist, but that what needed to be done was to see that it was carried on in better-suited places. Thus the great road races vanished one by one; even the Targa Florio, the classic race that has been run for more than fifty years on the tortuous Madonie circuit has now no option but to find a new circuit.

As the years went by, permanent circuits began to spring up. On these it was possible to accommodate the ever-growing numbers of spectators in proper enclosures, with essential facilities.

Realistically, therefore, this move towards track races to the exclusion of all others was irreversible. Thus, many automobile clubs took steps to establish new venues for motor sport events. As motor sport, helped by publicity and promotional effort, reached a new peak of popularity among the public and especially the young, the construction of a circuit seemed almost bound to be a sound and profitable commercial proposition.

Of course, it is not always easy to please everyone: while the drivers have taken action to increase safety margins on some of the new circuits built in the last few years, some enthusiasts have derided their efforts and accused

them of some sort of cowardice. This, then, is the problem facing the circuit planner: he has to stick to certain precise standards of safety and protection for the competitors and the public, and at the same time he has to design the circuit in such a way that it really puts the driver and his machine to the test. And it cannot be said that these two needs have in every case been satisfied.

According to the latest principles, a circuit has to offer, in technical terms, a track planned to cater for the future development of the racing car, and to take account of speed, trajectory, the strength of tyres and suspensions, and driver reflexes. Then there has to be an extensive network of auxiliary services: the pits must be properly located and planned, and so must the race control centre, the timekeepers' room, the press room, and the first aid centre. The plan must include provision for fire-fighting services, and for television and telephone link-ups to enable the race controllers to follow the sequence of events and to take immediate action when necessary.

Not least of the planner's concerns is the public, which has to be offered the best possible view for its money. This has led more and more planners putting into practice the theory that the best way of achieving this is to concentrate all the most demanding sections of a circuit into areas visible from grandstands. Because motor sport is no longer merely a means towards technological development and has become a spectator sport, it is only right that the spectator should get the maximum value for the money he spends on his ticket.

At this point it is worth mentioning safety aspects. Drivers have become more concerned about their own safety and that of their colleagues; they know exactly what risks to take and do not want to be forced to take unnecessary ones. For this reason the Grand Prix Drivers' Association several times has asked circuit owners to make the safety improvements that

Competition cars soon began to emerge as a breed quite distinct in appearance from normal road-going motors. Here is seen a group of Alfa Romeos at the start of a race at Monza.

Following pages: the frantic activity in the pits continued to draw crowds. The drivers themselves joined in to cut down the time spent out of the race. Here Tazio Nuvolari helps to refuel his Alfa Romeo.

In 1937 the most powerful Grand Prix cars ever built raced round the tight little Monaco circuit—here Caracciola and von Brauchitsch, both in 600-plus bhp 5·6 litre Mercedes W125s, lead Rosemeyer's Auto Union out of the chicane and along the harbour

The construction of permanent circuits by no means spelt the end of interest in the great road races. A classic of this *genre* was the Mille Miglia, which went halfway around Italy. The picture shows a Bugatti in action shortly after starting from Brescia.

Following pages: after the Second World War formula single-seaters began to race on circuits specially built for them. John Surtees is depicted here at the wheel of a Ferrari.

experience has shown to be necessary for the physical safety of both the drivers and the public.

The campaign carried on by the drivers has produced some real results, but it has also sometimes created severe difficulties for organizers committed to not inconsiderable expenditure by the improvements requested by the GPDA. More than once, in fact, these demands have resulted in circuits having to suspend racing altogether. The possibility that this sad state of affairs can arise means that, more and more often, planners of new circuits consult the drivers, especially on such matters as safety measures like guard rails and safety nets. This in turn has resulted in certain standards becoming established for safety precautions. New circuits are required to meet these

Circuits built according to precise safety standards are now the rule and are part of the world motor-racing scene. New ones are opened every year. Here Stewart's Tyrrell-Ford is being pressed by Emerson Fittipaldi's Lotus-Ford on the Buenos Aires circuit.

and their planners have to see to it that they do. Thus, once a circuit has
been designed, it has to be seen that the speeds possible, the width of the
track, the nature of the kerbs, the size of the run-off areas, the protection of
obstacles, the location of the pits and the protection of the public
enclosures, all contribute to the safety of the circuit.

Because circuits are the key to the present and the future of motor racing,
it is essential that they should guarantee both competitors and public a very
high degree of safety, one that is in practice hard to attain. For if there were
to be a repetition of the situation that brought about the disappearance of
the open road races, it would probably be impossible to find another
alternative.

Ten great circuits

Brands Hatch

The first sporting wheels that rolled on the land that became Brands Hatch were those of a group of cyclists led by Ron Argent, who, on their way home after a 125-mile tour in 1926, paused beside a fence bounding a huge, rolling field, dotted with mushrooms, that lay alongside the London–Dover road. For some years the area had been used for military exercises.

The cyclists clambered over the fence and asked the owner of a large nearby farm whether they might practise on their cycles along a track worn by the constant to-and-fro of farm wagons. He agreed, and Brands Hatch soon became a Mecca of cycling enthusiasts in the London area. The name, it seems, originates from the words 'de Brondehach', a thirteenth-century term deriving from Gaelic. 'Bron' means 'wooded slope'; 'hach', literally 'entrance to the forest'—and in fact the area is still densely wooded.

Argent and his friends in the cycling club spent a lot of their time there, often entire weekends. They would pause between long runs to rest in the shade of the lofty trees, and after a while an elderly couple converted an old army hut into a café to which the cyclists and their families could retire to eat and drink.

For two years cycling was the only sport that went on at Brands Hatch, and during that period the first race—a decidedly unusual one—was run; Jimmy Newson, a pioneer of the Woolwich cycling club, matched cyclists and cross-country runners against each other in a four-mile race. The runners against each other in a four-mile race. The runners won. Among the competitors was the Australian world champion, Jackie Hoobin.

At that time nobody dreamt that a day would come when the green, wooded landscape of Brands Hatch would echo to the roar of motor engines. Ron Argent, a young engineer fanatically devoted to cycling, just went on winning prizes—he was champion of Kent from 1933 to 1939, collecting over seventy trophies, most of them at Brands Hatch.

In 1928, however, the first motorcyclists tentatively essayed the rough track. They would wait patiently for the cyclists to finish circulating before racing round. Until the eve of the Second World War, Brands Hatch retained its character as a place for sport and recreation, but in 1939 the sportsmen abandoned their pursuits to take up arms, and the army moved back in, using the land as a vehicle park. During the long years of the war the area was the target of many a German bombing raid, and at the cessation of hostilities Brands Hatch was torn with gaping craters.

When the war was over, the bicycles stayed in the cellars, forgotten, and Brands Hatch became a venue for motorcycling events once again. Brands Hatch was soon able to offer a superb grass circuit, one of the best in Great Britain, and in 1947 a company calling itself Brands Hatch Stadium Ltd. was formed.

The course was improved by the construction of a wide earth terrace cut out of the hillside that slopes down to face the finishing straight, but efforts to asphalt the track, which was still a grass one, were scotched by the Ministry of Works, though the circuit's administration refused to accept defeat.

Meantime a new type of racing was thriving, the tiny F3 single-seaters powered by 500 cc motorcycle engines, with bullet-shaped bodywork. The arrival of these racing cars, such as those owned by John Cooper, Ken Carter, Ian Smith and Ken Gregory, made it imperative that the course be brought up to date, and the asphalting was finally carried out, at a cost, for the one mile, of £14 000—though not before Cyril Rogers closed the grass-track era with a record 59·6 mph on a motorcycle.

The first race on the new asphalt track was for motorcycles, and public attendance, at almost 35 000, was exceptional, but on April 16th, 1950—an historic date for Brands Hatch—the first car race was run. 10 000 spectators watched the day's racing and applauded the victories of Ken Carter, Don Parker and Bill Whitehouse. The course used was practically the same as today's club circuit, with the exception of Druids, and the cars went anti-clockwise.

A few months after the first competition, something was done that made Brands Hatch unique among British racetracks of the time. The closure of a racecourse at Northolt to make way for urban development of the area offered Brands Hatch Stadium Ltd. the opportunity of acquiring a large grandstand with considerable seating capacity. The structure was dismantled, transported to Kent and rebuilt along the central straight. Thus Brands Hatch took on an aspect not unlike that of the Continental racetracks, and one year later, still with the intention of improving the facilities, a telephone network was set up between the course marshals' positions and the central control. A small, well-equipped field hospital was also built, and gradually Brands Hatch began to look like a *real* racetrack.

Meanwhile both motorcycle and car races were being run. The circuit had been slightly lengthened and now measured almost 1¼ miles—too short, however, to allow any thought of accommodating bigger-scale activities.

When the company passed into the hands of Grovewood Securities Ltd., the Brands Hatch faithful told each other disconsolately that the land would be divided up and sold off, but in reality events took a much better turn, for the new company undertook considerable expenditure on improving facilities and on putting racing activities on to a more regular footing. After only a few years Grovewood began to make a good profit out of activities at Brands Hatch, thus confirming the value of their investment. Some time later, they handed over the management of the circuit to MCD, Motor Circuit Developments Ltd., under the direction of John Webb, who had previously been responsible for the circuit's public relations. Collaboration between Grovewood and MCD extended to other circuits as well: Mallory Park, Snetterton and Oulton Park.

The continuous process of improvements to the circuit itself and its facilities over the years now qualified Brands Hatch as a major international motor racing centre. The circuit, extended after construction work in the winter of 1959 to 2·64 miles with a minimum track width of 30 feet, lay ready for its glorious baptism, and in 1964 the great event took place.

It was decided that the British Grand Prix, which that year also carried with it the title of European Grand Prix, would take place at Brands Hatch instead of Silverstone. Previously the Aintree circuit had been used as the alternative to Silverstone, but, from 1964 on, Brands Hatch was to host the Formula One title race on alternate years.

That 1964 Grand Prix was a duel between Jim Clark (Lotus) and Graham Hill (BRM). This all-British struggle was an inspiring sight and Jim Clark's victory was acclaimed with a mighty ovation as the crowd released their pent-up excitement. The spectators had been able to follow almost all the stages of the race, thanks to the superb layout of the stands in relation to the track, which could be seen almost in its entirety by all those sitting on the terraces.

In preparation for the Grand Prix an illuminated scoreboard was erected which indicated the situation lap by lap, and a number of small shops were opened behind the finishing straight: Brands Hatch had entered the big league.

The alternation between Silverstone and Brands Hatch brought the top Formula 1 drivers back to Brands Hatch in 1966.

In common with the organizers of other major British races, Brands Hatch have always combined the Grand Prix with other races for lesser classes. Usually, at least one such race is run on the second official practice day and three or four on the day of the Grand Prix, thus offering real value for the price of a ticket and utilizing the circuit to the full.

In all, the public is offered a concentrated programme which fully repays the price of entrance and which includes various subsidiary entertainments to back up the big race.

In 1967, with the growing interest in long-distance races, Brands Hatch got its second international championship event; the 500-mile race for sports cars. The first of these resulted in a surprise win by Phil Hill and Mike Spence in a Chaparral, and since then the race has taken place regularly, though the 1973 race was skipped because of a big drop in spectator attendance in 1972. In fact the low takings of 1972 did not justify the considerable cost involved in organizing the title race in 1973, but it should be noted that the general falling-off of interest in motor racing during 1972 affected all the British racetracks and not just Brands Hatch.

As far as safety is concerned, Brands Hatch has not escaped criticism; some criticize the road surface, others claim that certain safety aspects are inadequate or ill-designed. In 1968 Stewart wrote; 'From the point of view of safety, Brands Hatch could certainly do with some improvements. The negative attitude of the Royal Automobile Club when we asked for protective nets in an area where there are trees with big trunks really upset me; in fact they told us that if we wanted the nets we, the drivers, could pay for them. As things turned out the nets were finally erected, and in other respects Brands Hatch needs only a few minor points attended to to make it a truly safe circuit.'

On October 24th, 1971, during a non-title race at Brands Hatch, the Swiss driver Jo Siffert, at the wheel of a BRM, lost his life. This tragedy aroused a great deal of controversy, one side claiming that the emergency services arrived too late and were useless, the other attacking the BRM, which trapped its victim in a blazing funeral pyre. Whatever the cause, it was a horrifying accident.

Perhaps spurred by this wave of criticism, Brands Hatch Circuit Ltd. put in hand a programme of improvements to safety measures at the beginning of 1972. An estimated £30 000 was spent on resiting the race marshals' posts, on enlarging some emergency run-off areas, on setting up additional metal barriers, and on remaking the kerbs along most of the track. All this work has helped to increase the safety margin for the many users of Brands Hatch, from international championship drivers to promising newcomers in the lesser classes.

Brands Hatch, about 20 miles from London, nestles among the green hills of Kent—a tranquil spot.

Major events draw big crowds to Brands Hatch. The English are notoriously keen when it comes to motor-racing, so even trade in posters is brisk. Among the most coveted are of course the ones specially produced for the race in question. The entrances are rigorously controlled. Every ticket bears the warning that those attending do so at their own risk.

The portly gentleman pictured above is one of the marshals. In the pits area there are numerous shops where the public can buy specialist publications, models and motoring kits. There is occasionally a uniformed band as well.

At most meetings the big race is not the only one offered. The organizers like to give the public a full programme; once having run a tractor race with the star drivers at the wheel.

One feature of Brands Hatch is that the paddock is quite separate from the pits, with a narrow tunnel linking the two.

During the hours before the big race the drivers take part in other forms of competition: on bicycles, as here, for example, recalling the cycling era at Brands Hatch. Some of the big sponsors set up refreshment centres for competitors and pressmen to make the waiting seem shorter. Then it's time to get on to the track, and the pits are thronged with people.

Another feature of Brands Hatch is that one can get to the inside of the circuit with one's car. In bad weather this means one can watch the racing, though at a distance, sheltered from the elements. It has also bred the popular habit of giving a long blast of one's horn to salute the victor as he makes his lap of honour.

The public can watch the racing from almost any part of the course. The outside of the circuit is lined with an almost uninterrupted row of grand-stands, and the purchase of a special ticket entitles one to visit many parts of the circuit, including the paddock, for which there is an additional charge. This gives one a chance to have a good look at the drivers and their 190-mph machines.

Emerson Fittipaldi

A lap at Brands Hatch

The first time I drove on the Brands Hatch Grand Prix circuit was when I had my Lotus 59 Formula 3 car in 1969. I think that Brands Hatch is one of the best circuits anywhere for a driver who really enjoys driving. The design of the circuit is good, with corners that go uphill and downhill . . . very interesting, and not just flat and featureless like some modern circuits.

Approaching Paddock Bend after a flying lap, it's very difficult to find the right braking point. Just where you want to start braking, there's a bad bump which unbalances the car. While braking you also have to start steering because the corner has already begun when you brake. You can't see round the corner until you've actually finished braking, and by then the ground is falling away very quickly, which tends to make the car understeer. Don't go too wide, or the car will never come back again! This point is very important, because you have to lift off the throttle for

a moment (at least that's what I do!) and try to put the car sideways down the hill. If you don't do this, the car starts to understeer badly under acceleration and can put you in big trouble. Most grand prix drivers understand the difficulties of Paddock Bend.

We all tend to go wide coming out of Paddock, in third gear, and you'll see a lot of people putting a wheel on to the kerb or in the dirt. They should have it sorted out as they go up the hill. The line through Druids is very much a matter of personal taste, but it is definitely the place to check your mirror because other drivers will want to pass under braking at Druids if they can, and it may be necessary to close the door on them. Normally I try to brake deep into Druids, then I just touch the apex and slide the car to the outside.

You mustn't let the slide get out of hand, though, because almost immediately you want to be on the right-hand side of

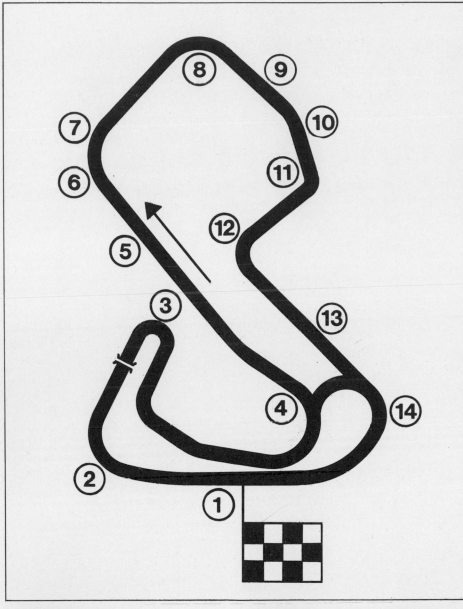

1 The long grandstand straight is not perfectly flat, and the finishing line comes at the end of a gentle declivity.

5 The fast stretch is characterized by Pilgrim's Drop, a dip. The car is suddenly lighter and then comes back to earth with a bang.

9 The first of the two successive bends that some drivers erroneously call 'esses'; this one is Dingle Dell, which is at the crest of a rise.

10 The entrance to Dingle Dell, which is linked by a very short straight with Stirling's Bend.

11 Heading for Stirling's the drivers brake heavily, change into 2nd, and come out of the bend in a controlled slide.

2 The entrance to Paddock Bend is the first delicate moment as it is essential not to drift.

3 After a short straight one goes into the next corner, Druids, which is an almost perfect hairpin; one has to brake hard for it.

4 After Bottom Bend and Bottom Straight comes South Bank, which is taken in a slight drift to put one into the right position to take advantage of the fastest part of the circuit.

6 Hawthorn's bend is a relatively fast ascending right-hander. The surface here is bumpy and decidedly tricky.

7 Leaving Hawthorn's bend, one comes on to the short Portobello Straight, which is taken in 4th gear.

8 The right-hander called Westfield precedes a stretch that hammers suspensions.

12 The entrance to Stirling's—here the drivers are braking in 2nd gear.

13 The straight before the big bend that leads to the finish; it passes under a bridge.

14 Clearways has to be very carefully judged as it tends to carry the cars outwards, off their trajectory.

the road, ready for Bottom Bend. This is another understeering corner, and you must have time to change up to third before scrambling across to the other side of the road. Bottom Bend presents no particular problems if you have got the car set up to oversteer on the way out. You should have it accelerating hard along Bottom Straight (which isn't straight at all, and is also rather bumpy).

The next corner, South Bank, offers a great challenge. Its main feature is that the radius tightens up on you half way round, so it is vital to enter it on the correct line; if you go in too wide, you'll never get back on line without lifting off. The part up to the bridge is taken in an understeer attitude, then you have to get the car sliding on the way out. If you can come out of here fast, you'll keep the speed all the way down the straight, which is the fastest part of the circuit.

As you go down the hill into Pilgrim's Drop, you get the same feeling that you have when you dive into a swimming pool: you feel the car almost falling down, and you hit the bottom of the dip very hard. The suspension hits all the bump rubbers and you can feel everything go solid for a moment. Almost immediately you have to brake for Hawthorn's, which is a climbing right-hander. Hawthorn's isn't particularly difficult, but it's bumpy. It's much faster than it looks, which means you mustn't brake too early, and then you can take fourth gear for the fast run into Westfield. After this there is another nasty dip to tax the suspension, and a fast kink which is just about possible flat-out unless the car is still on full tanks.

Then you brake hard for what I call the Esses: this is actually the fast right-hander at Dingle Dell followed by Stirling's, a tight left-hander. Dingle Dell is peculiar because you approach it uphill and can't see the apex. Instead you aim for the marshal's post (trying not to frighten the marshals), brake hard in third gear and try to get the car into a slide, playing with the throttle. For Stirling's you have to move from the left to the right across the road, and then brake very hard as you go into the corner. This is taken in second, with the car oversteering if possible, and you can help it by giving the steering wheel a quick jerk.

Now you can take third gear and hold it all the way back on to the 'club' section of the circuit, under the bridge and into Clearways. This must be approached exactly right because the road falls away on the outside and this can get you into big trouble. A moment's loss of concentration here gave me a nasty moment in my Formula 3 car in 1969.

You take fourth gear before you get to the pits, where there will be a signal telling you just how well you managed to do the previous lap.

Born in San Paolo, Brazil, on December 12th, 1946, Emerson Fittipaldi made a rapid rise to prominence, winning the World Championship in 1972. He came to England in 1968 and moved with almost disconcerting rapidity from Formula Ford into the Lotus Formula 1 team in the course of only two years. In 1974 he joined the Texaco-Marlboro McLaren team.

Buenos Aires

'Where just a few months previously a foetid swamp tainted the air on the edge of Buenos Aires, the international grand prix season began, in its search for the fourth world title-holder. Never before in South America had a motor course been raised to such an important position; and the *17 de Octubre* circuit gave the public, bursting with almost too much enthusiasm, everything they wanted.'

It was in these glowing terms that the 1953 Ferrari yearbook described Buenos Aires' entry into international motor racing. In fact the new racetrack had been opened in 1952, but at first only minor races were run.

As also happened in the cases of other South American tracks, Buenos Aires assumed more and more importance in line with the increasing prominence of Argentinian drivers in the international racing scene, among these latter being: Juan Manuel Fangio, five times world champion; José Froilan Gonzales, nicknamed 'Pepe' or 'Cabezon'; and Onofre Marimon, Fangio's favourite *protégé*. The presence of Argentinian drivers in official teams eventually led to Argentina being included in the round of title races.

International motor racing had begun in Argentina immediately after the war. In 1947, with the strong patronage and support of President Perón, three races for Formule Libre were organized: two consecutive Coppa Perón races at Buenos Aires (both won by Villoresi in a Maserati) and a third at Rosario, where Villoresi was beaten by Varzi in an Alfa Romeo, all three being road races. The idea of a series of consecutive races was a success, and in 1948 the series was repeated, this time with two races at Buenos Aires, one at Mar del Plata and one at Rosario. The series was christened *Temporada* as the races were run during a particularly hot time of the year.

In the meantime the Argentinian organizers had begun to realize that these races were open to a lot of criticism: the amount of spectators, and the fact that they swarmed on to the roads on which the races were being run, constituted extremely dangerous elements. A number of accidents punctuated these early races of the *Temporada*: in January 1949, during practice for the Coppa Perón, which was being run that year at Buenos Aires, the famous French driver Jean-Pierre Wimille was killed when his Gordini left the road—he had probably been dazzled by the sun.

Work on the construction of a racing circuit at Buenos Aires was begun, and in 1951 the Coppa Perón was run at Costanera, where Gonzales in a Ferrari won both the races in the programme, beating the 1939 Mercedes driven by Lang, Kling and Fangio. The following year the *Temporada* returned to Buenos Aires, this time to its brand-new track, which had been built to the highest contemporary standards. From that moment the focus of international racing in Argentina was the Buenos Aires track. The most important race, of course, was the Grand Prix, which was run every year from 1953 to 1958 without a break, the 1958 race being a milestone in motor racing history, for it was the first World Championship grand prix to be won by a rear-engined single-seater, Stirling Moss's Cooper-Climax. In these first years the public's leading idol was—naturally—Juan Manuel Fangio, who swept to victory in front of his fans in 1954 in a Maserati, in 1955 in a Mercedes, in 1956 in a Ferrari, and in 1957 in a Maserati.

On January 18th, 1953, during the first Grand Prix to be run on the *17 de Octubre* circuit (named after the date in 1945 on which Perón was released from captivity), a serious accident occurred: Farina's Ferrari went into an uncontrollable slide and hit some spectators crowding the edge of the track after breaking through the police cordon. The toll exacted by this tragedy was a heavy one: nine people killed and over forty injured.

The problem of spectators has been a continuous thorn in the side of the organizers of the Automobile Club of Argentina, who, though possessing a permanent racing circuit, have been unable to control the exuberance of the public. In the 1954 Grand Prix, Hawthorn was disqualified because of the presence of spectators on the track. After spinning off, the English driver was helped by some spectators to get his Ferrari back on the track; the marshals reported this incident back to the organizers, and Hawthorn was disqualified.

When the multiple champion Fangio and the other leading Argentinian drivers left the stage (Marimon died at Nürburgring in 1954) the Buenos Aires track entered a grey period; the last Formula One race to be run there was in 1960. The circuit continued to be used for national events, but exchanges with Europe became very rare, though in 1964 an effort was made to restore some of the old lustre to the *Temporada* by organizing a series of four races for Formula 2 single-seaters. There were not very many entrants, and victory went to Silvio Moser, who gained first place in the two races at Buenos Aires and in the rounds at Rosario and Córdoba. In 1966 Juan Manuel Fangio made a comeback, this time as organizer, to uphold Argentina's sporting banner. He organized a *Temporada* for Formula Three single-seaters, run at Buenos Aires, Rosario, Mendoza and Mar del Plata, and won by Charles Crichton-Stuart.

In the meantime a number of young, up-and-coming Argentinian drivers were beginning to make names for themselves, and the renewed interest in motor racing that their activities generated attracted the attention of the state petroleum agency, the YPF (Yacimientos Petroliferos Fiscales). In 1967 four Formula Three races were run, two at Buenos Aires, one at Mar del Plata and one at Córdoba, all won by Jean-Pierre Beltoise in a Matra.

In two *Temporada* races there were accidents involving both drivers and spectators, and it was therefore with relief that the Formula 2 drivers got a guarantee from Fangio that the 1968 *Temporada* would be run exclusively on permanent racing circuits. The victor that year was Andrea de Adamich, who won two races out of the four (two at Buenos Aires on circuits 9 and 6, and the others at Córdoba and San Juan). In 1970 the *Temporada* found a permanent home at the modernized Buenos Aires circuit, which, as a result of political changes, no longer bore the name *17 de Octubre* but the more simple appellation *Autodromo Municipal*. The competition was made up of two races, for 'sports-prototype' cars and 'sports cars' of Groups 5 and 6, and victory went to the Matra of Pescarolo and Beltoise and the Alfa Romeo of Courage and de Adamich.

There was a new meeting at Buenos Aires in January 1971. The 1 000 kilometres, a world championship sports car race, was marred by a major accident, involving Ignazio Giunti in a Ferrari and Jean-Pierre Beltoise in a Matra. The impact took place almost opposite the crowded grandstands, at the beginning of the straight. Giunti rammed the Matra, which Beltoise was pushing towards the pits, and in the blaze that ensued the Italian driver died. This tragedy caused a fierce controversy, not so much about the Number 15 circuit as about the conduct of the drivers of the race.

Whatever the cause, Buenos Aires municipality decided to modify the circuit and to carry out an extensive programme of works with the intention of offering the world championship circuits a venue among the best in existence.

The Number 15 circuit was partially rebuilt in 1972, with the construction of two 'esses', one after the bend before the pits, the other in association with Ascari bend, which was too fast and therefore too dangerous. Apart from these alterations, work was also done on the track surface, which was widened on the downward slope towards the grandstand bend, and raised kerbs were set on the outside of many bends to discourage drivers from clipping the edges. Small towers were erected to enable the marshals to follow the progress of the race and to signal to the competitors by means of a fixed system of lights. These lights took the place of signal flags, which are still used on most of the world's circuits.

Other work included the erection of a long guard-rail along one part of the track to protect one of the grandstands, though elsewhere it was thought preferable to leave large run-off areas. The pits were most radically altered; they were completely rebuilt and set further back, giving a deceleration lane separated from the track by a guard-rail. There are now more pits, and behind them are new garages for the cars. A highly up-to-date medical centre was also built, with an operating theatre, resuscitation equipment and all other aids, while emergencies on the track are catered for by a fleet of ambulances, each with a doctor, a nurse and a driver on board.

Just before the pits a modern timing tower was erected, complete with high-precision electronic apparatus, and above the pits a large air-conditioned press room was built. Today the Autodromo Municipal de la Ciudad de Buenos Aires is without any doubt a thoroughly modern establishment that meets the needs not only of the public and the competitors, but also of all those who live and work in the motor racing world.

The autodrome includes a number of circuits, each partly using the same stretches, but for the big international races it was decided—at the time when work was begun—to reserve circuits Number 9 and 15 for special purposes, and they have since been used respectively for the Grand Prix race and the 1 000-kilometre sports car race. The latter, begun in 1954, was run periodically until 1960. It was included in the calendar once again in 1970, but the 1973 race was cancelled due to lack of interest shown by Matra and Ferrari, as the world championship had already been clinched by the French team.

PRECIO
DE ENTRADAS

OFICIALES $ 150.-
MIXTO 150.-
GENERALES 20.-
ESTACIONAMIENTO 10.-

BOLETERIAS
Y VENTA DE ENTRADAS

OFICIALES - BOLETERIAS 9, 10, 11, 12, 13, 14
17, 18, 19, 23, 24, 25, 26, 29 Y 30
MIXTO - BOLETERIA 1
GENERALES - TODAS LAS BOLETERIAS
ESTACIONAMIENTO - BOLETERIAS 9, 10, 11, 12, 13, 14
17, 18, 19, 23, 24, 25, 29 Y 30

Above; one of the entrances of the Autódromo Municipal de Buenos Aires. Left; fire-fighting trucks, with all the equipment needed in case of accidents. The drivers' requests have made this equipment *de rigueur* on all the world's major circuits. On the right; steaks being cooked on a huge grill. Called *asado,* these are Argentina's national dish and make an ideal motor-racing snack.

Opposite page; top left, beautiful women are part of the international grand prix scene. These are acting as standard bearers. Top right and bottom, Argentinian police, armed with guns and smoke-bomb throwers, maintain order and keep spectators inside their enclosures. They evidently take their work seriously. Above and right, Brazilian crowds with flags and banners.

There is always plenty of interest going on in the pits during practice before the race. The picture on the left shows Ronnie Peterson waiting to go out in his Lotus. In the centre, local idol Carlos Reutemann's overalls hanging out to dry, and Peterson talking to team-mate Emerson Fittipaldi in the shade of a multi-coloured umbrella. At bottom, the grandstands packed with people during a race. Opposite, Denny Hulme in a McLaren and two BRMs in action, against a backdrop of Buenos Aires skyscrapers.

Cars racing past the pits and the race control centre. Note the illuminated board showing how many laps remain—a useful service for drivers and spectators. On the left, the victor celebrates his win; this time it's the Brazilian Emerson Fittipaldi.

Carlos Reutemann

A lap at Buenos Aires

Coming round on a flying lap of the Grand Prix circuit, I select top gear about half way down the main straight—just past the pits —and take a quick look at the gauges before beginning to turn about 100 yards before the corner. I normally begin to brake about 50 yards further on, then engage fourth gear and continue to ease the car into the corner. We are doing about 125 mph at this point, so it is important to have the line absolutely right—if you are on your own. This is one of the most popular corners for overtaking, and often it is necessary to go in a bit tight in order to shut the gate. The corner also tightens up as you leave it, so it is very important to stay in the middle of the road until about half way round. Then you gradually feed the power in until you see the point where the sports car circuit branches off, set the car up for a bit of oversteer and then accelerate hard out of the corner, clipping the piece of infield track.

Then there is a sharp burst down to the Ascari Curve, which I approach doing about 10 600 rpm in fourth gear. This is a very fast corner, and I usually brake at about the 100 metre mark. The Ascari is rather unique, in fact, because right in the middle of the corner the sports car circuit rejoins the Grand Prix course. This raises the level of the track at that point a little, and when you cross it the car gets very light. It also happens to be right on the apex of the corner, which usually makes things quite exciting. It doesn't alter your line, though, it just means that this is not a corner where you overtake or be off line. Coming out of the corner there are no kerbs on the outside, only grass, so it is important not to put a wheel off the track. I come out of Ascari at about 10 200 rpm in fourth, give the car a short burst of acceleration and then brake heavily at 100 metres for the first hairpin—another popular overtaking spot.

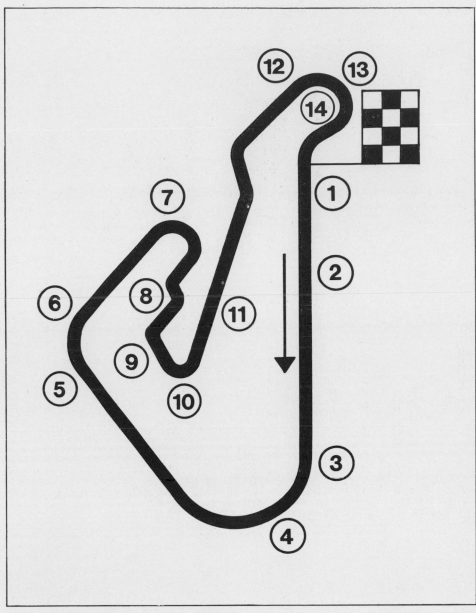

5 After a short straight one comes to Ascari bend, another fast one; the link with circuit No. 15 is here.

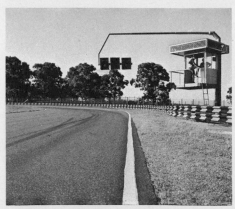

9 The first of the two left-handers that bring the cars on the stretch opposite the finishing straight. Here the drivers ease off the accelerator, while staying in 3rd.

10 After a 65-yard straight the second left-hander comes up, the drivers braking and still in 3rd.

11 The straight parallel to the finishing straight descends gently. Note the marshals' box with light signals.

2 The very broad straight passes a series of grandstands, then comes to the braking point for the first bend.

3 The entrance to Curvon, which is taken at 120 mph. Cars often overtake here.

4 Halfway round Curvon the bend gets tighter, which means that it is essential to set the car up right at the entrance.

6 Leaving Ascari the car hops on the uneven section where the two tracks join. The absence of kerbs makes it essential to keep the wheels on the asphalt.

7 The first corner on circuit No. 9 calls for hard braking: drivers generally drop straight from 4th to 2nd.

8 The esses immediately after the corner demand careful positioning, turning very late without drifting too much.

12 The entrance to the long final corner, which is preceded by a very fast left-and-right taken at full throttle.

13 The exit from the final corner, which is much faster than the one after Ascari. This stretch was intended to slow the cars down.

14 Immediately after leaving the corner there is one more bend, which leads on to the grandstand straight. The drivers change into 4th opposite the pits.

I go straight from fourth to second for this corner and position the car to the left of the track. It's a fairly late apex here, and it is very important not to drift too much to the left coming out of the corner because there is a quick left–right soon afterwards. If you come out of the hairpin too fast or on the wrong line you will not be fast through the sequence of corners ahead— you have to be thinking ahead all the time at Buenos Aires. I stay in second gear out of the hairpin, and through the esses, again not sliding too much to the left coming out. Then I select third before the two left-handers leading on to the back straight.

These two corners—and they are separate corners—are joined by a short straight, about 60 yards long. It is only necessary to back off for the first left-hander, and you can get back on the power about half way through the corner. I brake for the second one, which is much tighter, and I always make quite a late apex here, putting the power on in the middle of the corner and taking care not to clip the very high curb on the inside. I accelerate out in third on to the back straight, which is actually slightly downhill, and go into fourth before braking for the very fast left–right kink. I like to take the first part of the kink very tight with a late apex, so that I can come out of the second one very fast. Although both corners have about the same radius, the first one is actually taken much slower.

I stay in fourth gear through both of these corners and up to the second hairpin, which in fact is faster than the first.

It was here that Emerson Fittipaldi passed Cevert in the 1973 race, and I just don't know how he did it—I've never seen anyone overtake here before because it's so difficult to be close behind someone going through the kink. This second gear hairpin actually tightens up as you leave it, so again it's a late apex, and again it's important not to slide to the fullest extremity of the circuit. This is the new section of track built to slow the cars before the pits as a result of the Beltoise/Giunti accident. I accelerate out in second, change straight into third before the left-hander and then accelerate down the straight, selecting fourth gear opposite the pits.

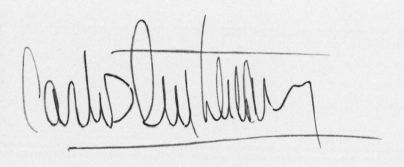

Carlos Reutemann, born at Santa Fé, Argentina, on April 12th, 1942, started motor-racing early, winning for three consecutive years (1966–1968) the national Touring title. Included in a team sent to Europe, Reutemann was the only one to gain a good footing in the international stakes, driving regularly in Formula 2 and later joining the Brabham Formula 1 team. He won his first Grand Prix in South Africa in 1974.

Indianapolis

Indianapolis motor stadium was born of the genius of four men who saw in the automobile the vehicle of the future. This was in 1908, when the first motor cars were driving around the streets of Indianapolis, and when the era of the bicycle—which had enabled Carl Fisher and Arthur Newby to achieve a certain degree of financial well-being—was drawing to a close. The idea came to Fisher, who proposed to construct a track on which motor races could be run and on which motor car makers could test their creations. Frank Wheeler and Jim Allison joined in this enterprise.

On February 9th, 1909, a company, the Indianapolis Motor Speedway, was founded, with a capital of $250 000. Fisher was elected President, with Newby and Wheeler as Vice-Presidents, and Allison as Secretary-Treasurer. The new company's first action was to buy 320 acres of land to the north-west of the city—and this set off the chain of events that led to the creation of 'the greatest motor course in the world,' as it was immediately dubbed.

Fisher planned two tracks, one of five miles, the other exactly half that distance. The four men got together, discussed the pros and cons, and finally agreed on the shorter track, which could be contained in a proper stadium with grandstands all the way round. Contemporary reports called it a 'bowl', or an 'oval', but in fact the track was a perfect rectangle, with four bends linked by four straights. The bends, 460 yards long, are slightly banked, at 16·4 degrees, while the North and South straights, at 1 100 yards, are longer than the East and West straights, which are only 220 yards long. The width of the track varies from a minimum of 52 feet on the straights to a maximum of 62 feet on the four bends. In all, the 'rectangle' measures $2\frac{1}{2}$ miles.

Once the layout had been finalized and the project launched, Indianapolis Motor Speedway gave orders for work to start. A surface of gravel and packed earth was chosen. On June 5th, 1909, while work was still in progress, the first competition was held. It was a balloon race, which had very little to do with racing cars, yet 3 500 people took their seats in the rectangle, while another 40 000 swarmed around the gates of the course, creating the first traffic jam in the history of Indianapolis.

The day of inauguration was set for August 19th the same year and construction work, which had been proceeding at a record pace, was finished by the day. When the crowds entered the huge enclosure they found the tar and gravel circuit, a landing strip for aircraft, forty-odd buildings, a number of wooden grandstands, and subways giving access to the centre of the course—all this on what so recently had been 320 acres of bare land. Everything had been perfectly worked out, but one fault soon made itself evident. The surface of the track was unable to withstand the pounding and tearing of the racers' wheels. It broke up, causing the first of the very long list of fatal accidents that has characterized the history of the Motor Speedway. The driver William A. Bourque, the mechanics Holcoln and Kelhun (in those days mechanics rode with the drivers) and two spectators lost their lives in two accidents which took place during the three days' competition that celebrated the inauguration of the course.

An uproar of criticism ensued, but the owners of the Motor Speedway were quick to act. They decided to remake the track surface completely using the then-common method of laying it with clay bricks. The job was properly done, with the advice of engineers and road-building experts—a team was even sent to Salem, Massachusetts, to inspect the wear and tear on a brick road surface that dated back to 1629.

Thus the most original track in the world was born, earning the nickname 'Brickyard' because it had used some 3 250 000 bricks. Legend has it that one of these bricks is made of gold, but the truth is a little different: the governor of Indiana laid a gold-plated silver brick in its place a few moments before the inaugural race on the new track. Work had been completed in 63 days—another record achievement—with the workmen laying an average of 50 000 bricks a day.

The first meeting on the new track was on December 17th and 18th, in bitter cold, when Louis Strang in a 200-hp Fiat set up some speed records; and from May 27th, 1910, for three days the Motor Speedway hosted a series of races, 42 in all. A 60 000-strong crowd guaranteed the financial success of the meeting, and there was an equally good turn-out for the meeting on July 4th.

In the meantime the four associates were trying to think of a way of spreading the name of their Motor Speedway throughout the world. First of all they decided to focus on one racing event with its own special characteristics, and they agreed on a 500-mile race with really good prize money. Then they examined the calendar and picked Memorial Day, the day of remembrance, for their race. Thus the famous Indianapolis 500 was born, known to most Americans simply as 'the 500'. The organization of this event was entrusted to T. E. Myers and Eloise Dallenbach. Entries were invited, positioning on the starting grid being based on the order in which entries were received.

The competitors were required to carry out a short preliminary trial in their cars, the principle being that only cars proven to be capable of more than 75 mph would be allowed to enter the race.

Forty cars took part in the first '500' on May 30th, 1911, when the race was won by Ray Harroun at the wheel of a Marmon Wasp. Inevitably, as it seemed, the race claimed its first victim, Arthur Greiner's mechanic Sam Dickson, who was thrown out after their Amplex car hit one of the protective walls. These walls, built for the protection of the spectators, are another of the Motor Speedway's special characteristics. Quite rightly, it was thought that the public should be safeguarded to the greatest possible degree, and reinforced concrete walls were built along the front of the grandstands. Scores of cars have crashed into these over the years, and often their drivers have been killed, yet nothing has ever been done to eliminate this danger to the competitors, who seem to be prepared to run unnecessary risks in order to win the race and the big prize money that victory brings.

The Indianapolis track has not changed significantly with the passing of the years, apart from being re-surfaced and the addition of new, more functional buildings. Indissolubly linked with the '500', the course has grown only in order to accommodate the ever-greater number of spectators, who come in a mad, teeming rush to watch the big race, in which courage and folly are linked.

The process of bringing the Motor Speedway up to date has been a continuous one, and the list of improvements is long even if one excludes things like the new grandstands, the addition of further subways, the enlargement of the pit area and so forth. In 1925 fire destroyed the 'Pagoda', a wooden building which housed the press and the race control centre, but one year later the Pagoda rose again, bigger and better equipped. In 1927 the founders of the Indianapolis Motor Speedway sold the entire establishment to the American air ace Captain E. V. 'Eddie' Rickenbacker, who, with the resolution and single-mindedness which only a true

sportsman could supply, took the course yet further forward, carrying out improvements even during the Depression that paralysed the United States.

In 1935 the track received a new and highly desirable accessory—a system of green and yellow signal lights which took over the race marshals' duty of signalling instructions to the drivers—and the same year crash helmets were made compulsory for all competitors. Between 1936 and 1939 a momentous change took place: the brick pavement disappeared, covered by a smooth layer of asphalt, though in memory of the famous 'brickyard' a short stretch of the finishing straight was left, remaining thus until 1961.

In 1945 the ownership of the Speedway passed into the hands of businessman Anton Hulman Jr, who has since made a substantial contribution towards maintaining the high standards of the Speedway and of the big race. By means of a long series of personal contacts, Hulman has drawn into the Speedway net many major companies in the motoring sector, with the result that the '500' is a meeting which they cannot afford to miss, either as protagonists or as sponsors. Among the many things done by Hulman during his reign, which continues to this day, were the replacement of the wooden grandstands with new ones made of steel and concrete, the resurfacing of the entire track between 1964 and 1969, and the erection of a big control tower in place of the old-fashioned 'Pagoda'; besides housing the race control centre, the timekeepers and the press, this tower has seats for 14 000 spectators. Then came the installation of big electronically-operated indicator boards showing the competitors' positions minute by minute: the most impressive is the one on the finishing straight, which gives all 33 drivers' positions, one on top of the other.

A number of safety measures have also been taken, like the rebuilding of the pits, the enlargement of the area in which the mechanics work—the latter in teams of eight mechanics to each competing car, capable of filling the fuel tanks and changing the tyres in 18–20 seconds—or the modification of the grandstands' protective barriers.

The list of works carried out at Indianapolis between 1909 and today, in fact, bears witness to the management's desire all along to offer the public first-rate entertainment—and they have plainly succeeded. The course now offers well equipped grandstands, a whole range of services and shops, a 27-hole golf course, a motel, and a special area where spectators can see the drivers and their cars close up. This is big business: on race days two million bottled drinks, a million hot dogs, and truckloads of chewing-gum, popcorn and icecream are sold.

For the price of a ticket one buys thrills—but one can be paying for tragedy too. Indianapolis is one of the racetracks that has claimed the greatest number of human lives in terms of drivers and mechanics, though the public, with rare exceptions, has always escaped injury. More than 60 lives sacrificed on the altar of the sporting spectacle pose the question whether there is any logical justification or explanation for what goes on at Indianapolis. And yet victory in the '500' is one of the most treasured hopes of all American racing drivers.

Road no. 16a, leading to the Indianapolis circuit, is well known to all American enthusiasts. Though the circuit is still some distance away, the giant mushroom-shaped tank with its legend helps to create the right atmosphere. On the right, all that remains of Indy's legendary brick track. These eight rows of bricks are beside the finishing line.

Every year the 500 attracts a wide cross-section of spectators, most of them young, which explains the strange garb of the old VW on the right. Souvenir stalls abound, but better business is done at the food and drink stalls, where you can eat well and cheaply.

The enthusiasts' mecca is Gasoline Alley, where the single-seaters are housed. Every garage posts its car's best average during practice. Prize-giving too is an attraction: it takes place before the day of the race, which is reserved for the big race alone. Every detail is catered for on the day, right up to going over the track with a vacuum cleaner.

To shorten the wait, the public in the grandstands is offered every kind of entertainment. Pride of place goes to the band led by the lovely majorettes. Meanwhile tension mounts in the pits as the minutes tick by.

The pace car which is to lead the 33 competitors round on their warming-up lap. In the back seat with the inevitable girl is the gigantic trophy, bearing the portraits in bas-relief of all previous winners. The grandstands are full, the cars on the track, everybody waits.

The race has begun. The cars roar round the 2·5-mile track, watched by thousands. The illuminated tower scoreboard shows the positions of all 33 cars and is a unique feature of Indianapolis.

Peter Revson

A lap at Indianapolis

If you see a picture of Indy from the air, you'll notice that all the turns look alike. They are all left-hand, of the same 90 degree radius, and they are all banked 9 degrees 12 seconds. But despite that each one is a little different in character—due to such things as the nature of the surface, the colour of the pavement or slightly different types of banking. When you approach turns at around 210 mph with an entry speed of around 170 mph you notice every little thing in the road, because you keep going over that same piece of road continuously; it's not like a road course where you have a lot of variety.

There used to be a bump in the middle of turn 1 which made it the most difficult curve, and although it was re-paved a couple of years ago you can still feel where it was. Turn 1 looks to be the narrowest turn when you approach it—the grandstands make it seem like a funnel. I stay about a foot away from the wall on the

right—I don't think it's really worth while to get all the way over—and because we have turbo-charged engines with a bit of throttle lag I don't brake as far into the apex of the corner as I would on a road course. The closer you get to the apex of the corner the more throttle response you need, in case you encounter some instability on the brakes or the car gets a little sideways. So the idea is to finish your braking a little early and pick up the throttle smoothly, to have it well underneath you before you get to the apex.

To brake from 210 mph to 170 mph I get on the brakes pretty hard but not for long, because the drag created by those big wings is tremendous and as soon as you back off you can really feel the deceleration. Geometrically my line is absolutely normal, but the turns are very long and it takes some acclimitization to find out where the apex is, because when you first approach the turn you can't see

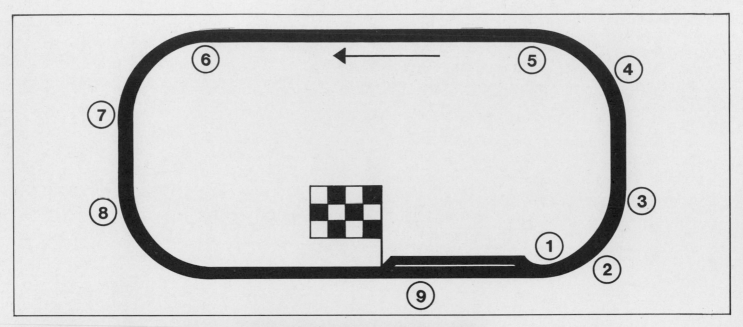

Peter Revson, born on February 24th, 1939 in New York, heir to a very wealthy family, drove in his first race in Hawaii in 1960. In 1963 he made a brief appearance in Europe, driving a privately-owned Lotus in Formula One. After returning to the United States he made an excellent reputation for himself in Can-Am races and joined the international circus in 1970 with the McLaren team, for which he won Grands Prix. He was killed while testing a Shadow at Kyalami in 1974.

1 The entrance to the first of the four corners seems the narrowest because the big grandstands overshadowing it make it feel like a tunnel.

2 Leaving the first corner. At this point the cars are already accelerating back towards peak revs.

3 The very short straight leading to the second corner. One accelerates hard on it and then brakes briefly but firmly for the corner.

4 Leaving the second corner one lines up for the straight opposite the grandstand straight, with one's car only inches from the outside wall.

5 This long straight is the fastest if the wind is behind one. If it is, one can get as much as 300 extra revs from the engine.

6 The beginning of the third corner, generally considered the most difficult of the four. On the inside the surface is irregular.

7 The second short straight, leading to the fourth and last corner, presents no particular difficulties.

8 The entrance to the last corner, considered the best of all because it has recently been resurfaced.

9 The exit from this corner is a popular place for overtaking bids. The finishing straight runs alongside the row of pits, which are protected by a low wall and a strip of grass.

the exit. I get the power on early—before the apex—because on a really high-speed corner you can loose a lot of time if you go in just a little slow. You get a perspective of where you should be on the corner, you're mind is ahead of the car, and after a lot of practice you know where you're position will be coming out: it's usually a foot or so from the wall.

We normally just feather the throttle before going into turn 2, and then it's flat out all the way round and out on to the back straight, which may or may not be the fastest part of the course depending on which way the wind is blowing. If the wind is blowing fairly briskly, say 15–20 knots, then it's going to give you 300 rpm more on one side than the other.

I find turn 3 the hardest. I don't know why, but for me it seems to be the most difficult. Maybe it's the approach, it just seems to be narrower than the other turns and also the inside verge is quite bumpy. It always seems as though I'm going into the turn too early. The track also seems to rise from the apex to the exit, as if there's a crowd at the exit. At the other turns the entrance level is the same as that of the exit, but at turn 3 you hit the apex and then the road seems to rise to a crown and levels off. The whole thing, of course, is very slight, but at those speeds you notice everything—even if it's only a six inch change in the terrain. The track levels off between the turns—not like Ontario where the banking is carried on to the short straights—but at Indy, because the track is so old, the curve banks, then flattens off, and then banks again. So in turn 3 it feels like the exit is more abrupt when it flattens out—it almost feels like a crown in the road.

Turn 4 is good. It was re-paved a couple of years ago and is probably the fastest turn of all—probably faster than turn 2. Coming out of this corner is also my favourite overtaking spot. Here you can either get a jump on someone or outbrake them into turn 1. You come off the turn, slingshot them, and then you can either pass them going down the front straight or try to outbrake them. If you do get inside someone going into turn 1 or turn 3 your entry isn't quite as good, because you're going in much shallower and you need to brake a little harder. But the point is that if you have been trying to get past a guy who is marginally faster—or marginally slower—he isn't going to re-pass you once you're on the inside unless you really go through very slowly. It's difficult to pass marginally slower cars now, because when you get up behind a slower car you lose so much road-holding efficiency due to the big wings losing their adhesion in the draught of another car; all of a sudden you're forced to do the speed he's doing, even though you're travelling a lot quicker on your own.

You get used to the speeds involved. You are constantly accelerating up to that speed and then decelerating—you are not maintaining the speed for a long time like you do at, say, Le Mans. It is possible now to go round at 190 mph without braking, but to my way of thinking you have to use the brakes to lap at 200 mph. Of course, you have to know how to use them—and that's where road racing experience comes in handy because I'm used to using the brakes as effectively as possible. Some of the Indy regulars have never really put much of a premium on brakes. Some of them insist that they go round as fast as they do without brakes—perhaps they do—but I still think that if you can use them properly you can save some time. For one thing it means that you are off the throttle for less time than if you're coasting. I maintain that the fastest way round Indy is to use a little brake—but only going into turns 1 and 3 because across the short chutes into 2 and 4 you don't use any brakes at all—you only feather the throttle for an instant. However, with tyres improving the way they are, we might be able to go flat out from 1 into 2 and from 3 into 4.

I try to set the car up as neutral as possible. I probably run less understeer than most people, but I definitely avoid oversteer—a car which is a little loose at the rear end will almost certainly be slower than one that is understeering slightly.

The track owners do a very good job in maintaining the surface—I think the last time it was re-paved was in 1971—and it's probably better now than it's ever been. As you know, they have one strip of bricks across the start/finish line just for the sake of nostalgia, and you can feel them every lap!

Kyalami

Motor sport has a passionate following in South Africa, and the numerous circuits there not only give local drivers a chance to unleash their enthusiasm, but also attract the international stars. Many of these circuits are well designed and well made, and would be worthy of a place in the international scene if only for their excellent supporting organization. Among them Kyalami stands out. It takes its name from a piece of land that borders the northern area of the circuit and which, in the Sesotro language, means 'my house'. The idea of creating this circuit came to a band of enthusiasts living in the Johannesburg area who wanted to find a new venue for the motor sporting events that took place at the Grand Central Circuit. This was a rather obsolete circuit which could no longer meet the needs of a constantly developing sport, where cars became faster every year. It was also a sport that was capturing ever more public attention, and the public demanded a bigger circuit, with more creature comforts.

Alex Blignaut, one of South Africa's leading exponents of motor sport, carried out an in-depth study of the commercial possibilities of an enterprise based on motor-racing activities, and calculated the investment that would need to be spent to build a truly modern motor-racing circuit, offering a track, buildings and facilities equal to or even better than the great European and American circuits.

The consortium represented by Blignaut initially focused their attention on a piece of land in the neighbourhood of Alberton. The area had been carefully examined and its potential evaluated, and the conclusion was that it offered all the requisite features. But then someone proposed an alternative location, pointing out that the Baragwanath area was even more suitable.

All this was watched with great interest by the motor sporting fraternity in South Africa, and by those living in and around Johannesburg in particular. The latter were extremely anxious to have a new circuit, and the prospect of taking away from East London the premier position among international racetracks in South Africa was by no means the least appealing factor.

At this stage the Mayor of Johannesburg, Dave Marais, stepped into the picture. A keen sportsman, he wanted to get through the planning and organization of the project as rapidly as possible so that the work of construction could be given the go-ahead with the minimum of delay. He therefore called a meeting of all the parties that had shown interest in the construction of a racetrack near the city and set out to find a solution that would satisfy everybody. If he did, he could then count on the backing of a single group with sufficient resources to finance the construction of the circuit. The first meeting was held in January 1961, at which the Presidency of the South African Motor Racing Club was awarded to Francis Tucker, Alex Blignaut being nominated Secretary. His job was to keep the various threads of the groups' interests knit together, while a sub-committee initiated researches into the all-round suitability of various locations for the construction of the new circuit.

As a result of the sub-committee's deliberations Kyalami was proposed, at a site in a hilly area about 15 miles from the centre of Johannesburg. When Tucker and Blignaut first suggested this it was rejected; but the two men were convinced of the advantages it had to offer and they campaigned hard to have it accepted. The ensuing debates and arguments were long and complex, but in the end Tucker and Blignaut got their way.

By this time the club had secured a number of major five-year contracts from far-seeing sponsors who believed in the future development of motor sport as a source of industrial and technological information. The task of building the new circuit was entrusted to the supervision of Basil Read, another man with boundless enthusiasm for motor racing, who put everything he had into the planning and construction of the track.

Working from a comprehensive study of the world's principal circuits supplied to him by Shell, Read decided to use a particular type of surface dressing on the track which gave excellent adherence in all weather conditions. He carefully studied the configurations of various existing circuits in order to be able to endow Kyalami with certain individual characteristics that were unique unto themselves and were not merely copied from existing examples. In addition—and very sensibly—he decided to give maximum consideration to the needs and interests of the public, which had not really been adequately attended to at the circuits already in use. Thus it was that the Kyalami circuit emerged not so much as a motor racing and technological research laboratory, but as the child of one man's conviction of the spectator attraction of motor racing. A premium was therefore put offering the paying public the best possible view of the racing; its founders considered this should be the main aim of a motor-racing circuit.

Kyalami's first races were run on November 4th, 1961, when the National Championship Rand Spring Trophy and the Nine Hour Endurance Race were contested.

Public attendance on the day was enormous, thanks largely to the excellent location of the circuit, relatively near to Johannesburg, Pretoria and the residential complex of Witwatersrand, while the spectators' ability to follow the competitors' progress around two-thirds of the course immediately won their approval of the new circuit.

The Nine Hours, an endurance race which was to gain international recognition, was run on the Kyalami circuit on its inauguration day in 1961, and since that year, which saw the fourth Nine Hours, it has remained a fixture in Kyalami's annual programme. Today it is known simply as 'The Kyalami Nine Hours'. It is worth noting that though the race had always been started like the great 24 Hours of Le Mans—that is to say with cars lined up on one side of the track and drivers on the other, and with the drivers sprinting for their machines at the drop of the flag—a new variant on this procedure was instituted in the interests of safety. The Royal Automobile Club, under whose aegis South African motor racing had operated since 1961, decided to abolish the traditional Le Mans start as being too dangerous, and to substitute a starting procedure in which the drivers are seated behind the wheels of their machines, fully strapped in, and their team-mates are lined up on the other side of the track, holding the ignition keys. At the starter's signal they run across to hand the keys to the waiting drivers.

Between 1961 and 1966 the circuit's popularity grew steadily, and many refinements were effected. Covered grandstands were erected and services also were improved. Finally, in 1966, came the announcement that Blignaut had always waited for: the South African Grand Prix would no longer be run on the East London circuit, as the organizers had decided that a 'world' fixture of this sort was too onerous a responsibility for them. Thus it was that the Formula One Grand Prix, which had been inserted into the international calendar in 1965 and which had been run at East London that year and in 1966 (though not being valid for the title) came to Kyalami in 1967.

The CSI sent a team of experts to carry out an on-the-spot examination of the circuit so that the teams competing in the World Championship could be guaranteed that the circuit and its organization were of a standard adequate for its regular use for the Grand Prix. The verdict was affirmative, though a suggestion was made to the circuit's owners that the track should be widened to bring it into line once and for all with international regulations.

Blignaut and Tucker, taking advantage of the mood of satisfaction created by the circuit's acceptance, obtained the consent of the council of the South African Motor Racing Club to carry out work additional to that suggested by International Sports Commission's experts. As a result of this the track was widened to 12 yards, and to 13·3 yards on the stretch from the Kink to Crowthorne bend, i.e. on the grandstand straight. This was a particularly wise measure. In addition the surface was relaid, as the dressing used when the circuit was first made proved rather hard for the latest racing tyres, while steps were taken to level the pit support area and to improve spectator safety precautions in line with modern world standards. The central grandstand was dismantled and re-erected further back from the track, and a bridge connecting the outside of the circuit with the inside was put up in the grandstand area (as on so many other circuits, this was a 'Dunlop bridge').

This programme of works brought the Kyalami circuit right up-to-date and the international star drivers soon expressed their appreciation of it. In 1968 Jackie Stewart made a merciless critical analysis of Grand Prix circuits, but had this to say of Kyalami: 'This is a circuit managed by extremely enthusiastic people, who listen to us and understand our requirements; Blignaut has transformed Kyalami into an excellent circuit and has balked only at putting up nets in place of the guard rails.'

With the passing of time Blignaut has altered his views of this particular safety aspect, and today Kyalami has tall, cleverly staggered safety nets to protect the public and to catch any cars that may run off the track, without, however, smashing them on impact. The Grand Prix Drivers' Association has expressed satisfaction with the way the South Africans have done things by several times awarding the circuit first place in their annual survey of circuits.

The secret of the Kyalami organizers' success lies in their constant and attentive watch on developments in the international motor-racing scene, which has prompted them to keep their circuit right up-to-date in every respect. Kyalami is considered to be a very safe circuit and no really serious accidents have yet occurred during big international races run there.

The Springbok Radio Tower houses the principal services and the radio and television link-ups. It stands on the inside of the track, facing the central grandstands, and is an excellent vantage point, offering a view not only of the finishing straight but also of work in the pits and the other side of the circuit from Jukskei bend to Clubhouse bend.

Opposite page, top; one of the circuit's emergency fire-fighting vehicles; centre left, the prize-giving area. Bottom left; a novel use for the protective netting. Bottom right; even children can be useful for advertising, especially when perched on an adult's shoulders.
Top; the back of Dave Charlton's transporter. He is sponsored by a cigarette manufacturer. Above; near nudity is fashionable at Kyalami, and is justified by the intense heat. Right; three track marshals, colourfully turned out.

Drivers share a joke. From the left; Revson, Stewart, Cevert, Scheckter (2nd row), Emerson Fittipaldi, Pace, Regazzoni and Beltoise. On the ground, Hulme, Peterson and Follmer. The picture on the left shows some enterprising spectators who have found themselves some 'grandstand' seats.

Spectators watch the proceedings and shelter from the sun on home-made grandstands. Below left; Denny Hulme's Yardley McLaren in the pits, with each mechanic doing his allotted task. Below right; Jackie Stewart waits.

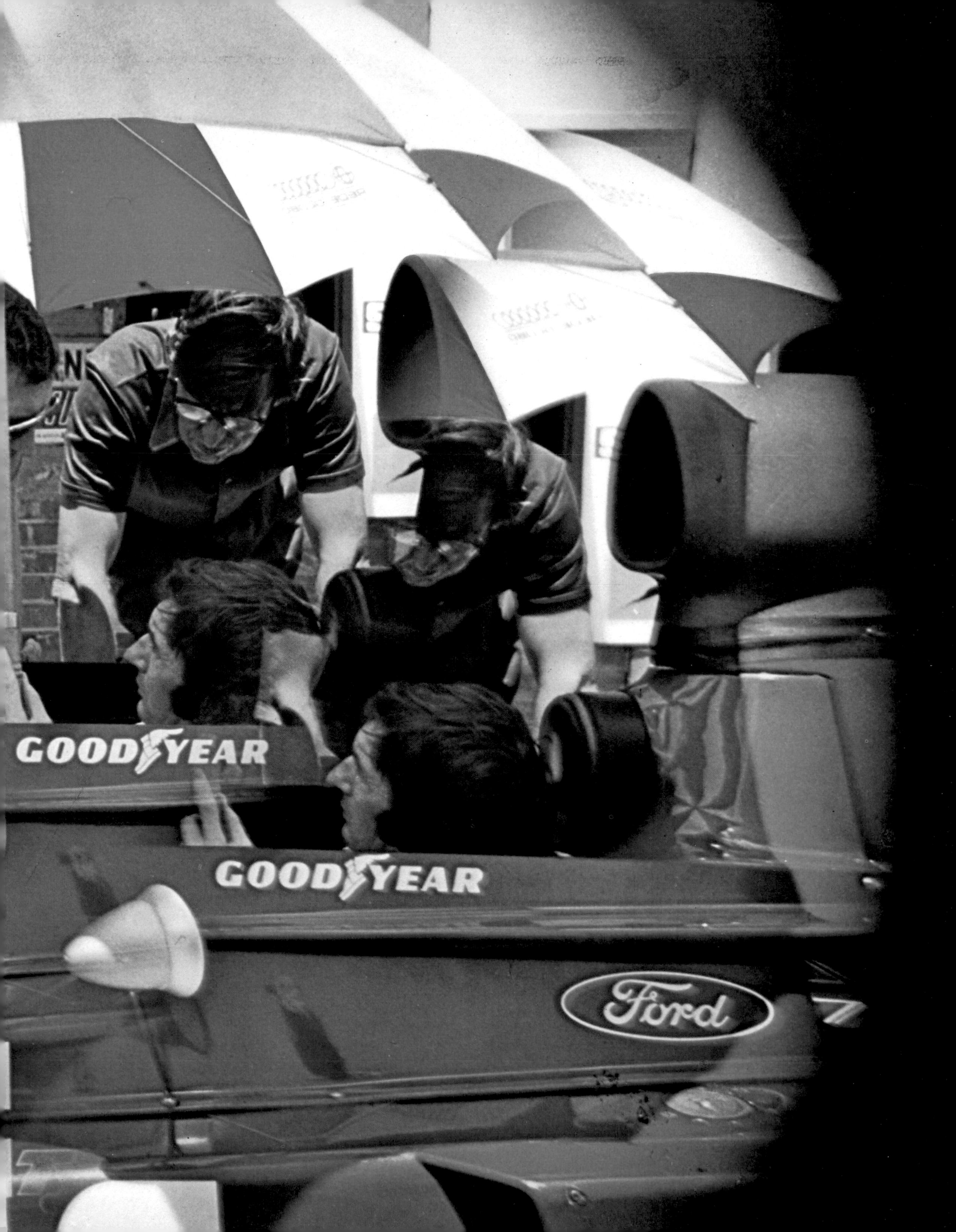
GOODYEAR
GOODYEAR
Ford

Preceding spread; Stewart seen chatting with his crew. This page, top; the race is on, with McLarens leading the field. Left; the McLarens first into Crowthorne. Above; tension relieved after 79 laps, the victorious Stewart, with a garland round his neck, sprays champagne over fans and photographers.

Denis Hulme

A lap at Kyalami

On a flying lap I select fifth gear about half way between the kink and the start/finish line. After this it doesn't seem to make too much difference which side of the road I run on down the straight, so I head under the bridge towards Crowthorne Corner. Approaching Crowthorne there is a filter lane painted on the road consisting of some dotted lines and solid white line, and I brake where the solid line stops turning left—at the 200 or 250 yard marker I believe. I go straight from fifth gear into third, braking lightly and then heavily in the middle of the braking area and then lightly again. The car then seems to speed up due to the reduction in g-loading, although, of course, it's still slowing down. At this stage I'm about half a car's width from the left of the circuit; you could go down the inside and brake at the same point, but you obviously get a better run down the hill towards Barbeque if you stay wide.

I let the brakes off and the car 'rolls' through Crowthorne very quickly in third gear. Our third gears are very high at Kyalami, so I have to get the corner very clean and accurate: in the race with a heavier fuel load I would probably use second gear, but you can just get away with the high third gear that McLaren run. I round Crowthorne, and there's a kerb on the outside which I try and brush; I do not like running up on it because it doesn't seem to give much adhesion. I put the power on after I'm about one-third of the way round the corner, feeding it on gently, but *all* of it.

After touching the kerb I select fourth gear and then set the car up for Barbeque Bend. The car initially labours in fourth at about 8 000 rpm but soon picks up on the downhill run. If you get Barbeque absolutely right then the left-hander that follows it, Jukskei, can be taken 'flat'—but it's very difficult. The car always understeers

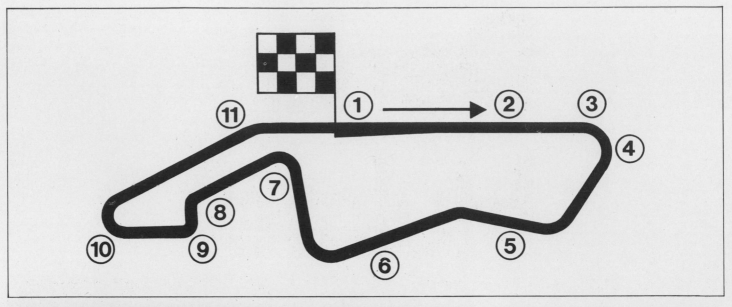

New Zealander Denis Hulme was born in Te Puke on June 18th, 1936. He drove in his first race in 1959 and made his Formula 1 début in 1966 with the Brabham team. He was World Champion for 1967, winning the title in a Brabham, and went over to the McLaren Grand Prix and Can-Am teams the next seasons.

4 Emerging from Crowthorne one comes to a very short straight ending in Barbeque bend. At this point one is already in 4th.

8 A tricky spot: the esses, a left-hander followed immediately by a right-hander leading uphill.

1 The grandstand straight, near the finish. The white markings on the track indicate starting-grid positions. In the background the top of the Dunlop bridge can be seen.

2 Having passed under the Dunlop bridge one goes fast downhill towards Crowthorne bend. There are grandstands on the outside of the bend as well as the inside.

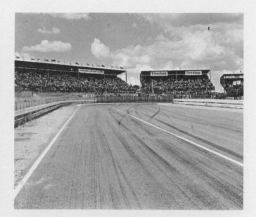

3 The big grandstands at Crowthorne. Here one drops to 3rd, having entered the bend keeping as far as possible from the outside of the straight.

5 After Barbeque bend there are two straights with a very fast bend between them. This is called Jukskei and is approached well to the right to enable one to take it at full throttle.

6 Now one descends rapidly towards Sunset bend, which is taken at speed in 3rd.

7 After a short burst another bend looms up: this is Clubhouse, which calls for a change down from 3rd to 2nd and exactly the right amount of accelerator when leaving.

9 The entrance to the second bend in the esses: they differ in radius and gradient. One brakes hard before them in order to accelerate through them.

10 At the exit from Leeukop corner one is confronted with two large grandstands full of people. This is a rather slow and difficult corner.

11 The last bend before the finishing straight is called the Kink, because it rises and then dips. It is not difficult, though one has to be careful not to go into a drift.

through Barbeque, but sometimes worse than other times. You've got to back off for just a fraction to let the front settle down and get some grip and then run flat-out round the corner, going very wide on the exit and thus making the two corners one continuous double bend.

Continuing flat-out in fourth, I cut back after Barbeque to about the centre of the track: my exit from Barbeque is so late that I really don't have too much time to get right over to the other side of the track and then come into the apex of Jukskei. The car turns very easily in the middle of the road before Jukskei but the big problem arises about half way through Jukskei; there you have to make a quick decision as to whether the car is going to be all right when it gets to the outside of the track.

Then, depending on the gear ratios, we run all the way along to Sunset in fourth gear. We sometimes go into fifth on the run to Sunset but when I'm qualifying I don't bother—I just run it up to about 10 300 in fourth. My braking for Sunset varies. There is a marker on the left hand side of the road which I use, and it's ideal if you don't brake too hard because that upsets the car. Any sign of a locking wheel tends to send you straight on. So I brake, let them off again and approach the corner with the car settling down again.

Sunset is taken in third gear, and is very, very fast. I stay about six inches from the kerb on the inside all the way round and watch the exit for a kerb that really disturbs the car—and try to avoid it! But you need to use as much of the road as possible, and ideally just nick the kerb.

I select third gear about half way along the straight after Clubhouse and then head up the hill towards the esses. I brake for a very short period just before the first corner, then let the brakes off to get the nose back in the air before the corner. The first corner appears to have an adverse camber, but it may not. I get a lot of power on in the first part of the esses, then quickly back off to let it roll round the right-hander with the car appearing to understeer. The nose dips in the middle of the esses, letting the car 'sink', and then I quickly get back

on the power again for the right-hander.

I then watch the road right at the end of the corner because the car slips and slides through the right-hander—sometimes understeering, sometimes oversteering. But by watching the kerbing at the end of the corner I can judge whether it's all going to be all right. So we honk on up the hill towards Leeukop. This corner also appears to be adversely cambered, but, again, it's not. Most drivers rush up to it on the left hand side of the track, brake in a straight line and then ease into a fairly late apex. I take a completely different line. My approach is the same but at the point where the others are just starting to brake, I pitch the car to the right, brake straight towards the corner, select second gear and then put the power on. The back doesn't break away during the 'pitch' because the braking ratio is mostly on the front wheels and I gain a lot of time on the other drivers who turn in later. My line is shorter, and its certainly a lot quicker. Once into the corner, I get off the brakes and start feeding the power on. Sometimes it starts to oversteer quite badly, sometimes it's quite neutral—I think it just depends on how hard I'm trying. I try to just ever-so-lightly touch the kerb on the inside and then accelerate over to the outside of the corner without too much wheelspin or sliding around. If everything is organized and the wheels are just vibrating—the tyres trembling—I know I have got the right amount of power on. This is the corner where we feel the most vibration, because it is one of the slowest, it's uphill and it's the one where you try and put a lot of power on to get a run home. Right at the end of the outside kerbing I go into third at 10 300 rpm, then fourth about half way down the straight before the kink (at 10 300 rpm), and then fifth at 10 400 rpm if I'm really in a hurry. The kink is no problem, but I try to touch the kerb on the inside and then let it run out on to the dirt on the outside: it takes a lot of sideload off the car, and sideload slows a car down.

The end of the straight is one very easy place for overtaking, and you can also pass going into Sunset Bend.

Le Mans

Though in design and construction vastly different from Indianapolis, the Le Mans circuit has many points of contact with the American one. Like Indianapolis, for example, Le Mans exists for one major annual event—the 24 Hour Race. For the French, Le Mans is a sort of national sporting symbol—almost more so than Indianapolis is for the Americans—but perhaps this is due to the unique patriotic fervour of the French, which some even consider chauvinistic.

Originally conceived for the most worthy motives, such as technological research into the development of the motor car and experiments with new road services to cater for its new needs, Le Mans has gradually lost its exalted technological significance and has moved on to a more materialistic and commercial plane, this as a result of the realization that the 24 Hours was attracting some of the best racing drivers and sports cars and an ever-increasing spectator attendance. This is true of other circuits as well, for modern technology now has other means of research and trial at its disposal, and the survival of a circuit is now largely dependent on the quality of the entertainment and sport that it has to offer. At Le Mans it has been conclusively proved that the 24-hour race has a strong public appeal. Others have organized duration races, following in the footsteps of the Automobile Club de l'Ouest (ACO), but, as always happens with imitations, the original is still the best.

The circuit and the race, therefore, have been inextricably linked throughout the history of Le Mans. The story begins on October 9th, 1922, when Georges Durand, secretary of the ACO, opened a letter sent him by Emile Coquille, director of the French subsidiary company of Rudge Whitworth Wheels. Coquille offered 100 000 francs to help the ACO to organize a race, though in effect he was really making a concrete offer of prize money, knowing, from the ACO's excellent record of organizing sporting events, that he could trust them to do the right thing.

This proposition naturally took Durand by surprise, not so much because of the sum offered, but the completely free hand he had been given in the choice of the type of race it was to be. Suddenly, a tremendous idea occurred to him—and a few days later Durand, the journalist Charles Faroux, the ACO president Gustave Singher, and two officials, Verney and Canit, met around a table. The idea of a Grand Prix was rapidly discarded and talk centred on the possibility of a long-duration race. Some were for a 1 000-kilometre race, others advocated a 12-hour contest. Faroux was the boldest and suggested a 24-hour race, supporting his proposal by emphasizing the value of the opportunity this would offer motor car manufacturers to identify and sort out all the problems raised by the need to keep a car going for an entire day without a stop. When the meeting broke up, a positive decision had been taken to launch the contest that Faroux had proposed.

Faroux, as the proposer of the race, was to draft the regulations; the others got down to sorting out the administrative details. As a circuit they chose one used by the ACO in 1919, which was triangular in shape and measured 10·71 miles: from Pontlieue to Mulsanne, then a stretch in the direction of Arnage, followed by a curve that turned right round to lead back to the start along other bends and straights. Broadly, the circuit used today is the same as was used then, though a large number of modifications have been made.

The rules worked out by Faroux were extremely precise and rather strict. These stipulated the use of normal production cars, exactly as those advertised in the manufacturers' catalogue for that year, and immediately guaranteed a strong interest in the race from motor car manufacturers as well as the general public, who would be able to witness a severe test of the cars that they could buy the next day. To cite a particular example, the regulations specified that all the competing cars should arrive at the start with their canvas hoods erected, and that the drivers should lower these before moving off. It was because of this that mechanisms for erecting and lowering hoods were rapidly improved and refined.

The first 24-hour race was run on May 26th, 1923, and 33 cars of 18 different makes set out over the roads of water-bound macadam. These were the public roads that linked Mulsanne and Pontlieue. At the point where there is now the bend after the grandstands on the finishing straight the road went straight on towards Pontlieue in the suburbs of Le Mans to join the main road to Tours. The race was a success, won by Lagache and Léonard in a Chenard-Walcker. In the 24 hours they had covered 1 732 miles, at an average of a little over 57 mph. No fewer than 30 cars of the 33 starters crossed the finishing line, which must be a record.

In 1926 a fierce argument broke out between the organizers and the owners of the land on which the various installations were being built. Without hesitation the ACO transferred the grandstands and the pits to another location, near a racecourse adjacent to the track. This trouble, however, soon blew over, for in 1926 everything went back to its old position after financial agreement with the landowners had been reached.

The Le Mans circuit has remained practically the same throughout, but it has undergone a long series of minor adjustments. In 1926, the same year as the grandstands and pits went back to their original locations, the Pontlieue–Mulsanne stretch was asphalted and other sections were resurfaced, while car-parks for 3 000 vehicles were built. In 1929 the first modification, albeit slight, was made to the configuration of the circuit. The hairpin bend at Pontlieue was no longer adequate for the demands of the race, and the ACO therefore decided to cut it out by creating a link road between the Pontlieue road and the Mulsanne–Tours road, thus skipping the centre of the suburbs. The new stretch, called the 'Rue du Circuit', left the Pontlieue road 440 yards before the houses began and joined the Route

Nationale to Tours by means of two right-hand bends. This made the circuit about 1 100 yards shorter, reducing it from 10·71 to 10·14 miles. As the years went by the renown of the 24-hours spread ever wider, and competitors from all over the world came to take part. In 1931 the Italians had their first victory, won by the Howe-Birkin Alfa Romeo, and in the same year the race claimed its first spectator victim, who was knocked down by a Bugatti. Seven years before, the driver Mestivier had lost his life when his Amilcar left the road at Hunaudières.

1932 was a decisive year in the history of Le Mans. The new link road had failed to solve all the problems; though it avoided the suburbs of Pontlieue, the stretch of road that led to the Rue du Circuit was too narrow and difficult, and both racing drivers and the public were subject to needless risks because of the reduced width at this point. The ACO decided to buy a piece of land extending from the pits to the road to Mulsanne, and by laying a new stretch of asphalt 1 645 yards long, the pit area was joined up with the long Mulsanne straight via a series of bends. This reduced the circuit by a further 3 114 yards to 14 755 yards.

Considerable improvements had taken place in techniques of road building, and the new stretch was designed and laid by the latest methods. It was sunk below the level of the surrounding land in order to give the public a better view and better protection, for between them and the track was an earthen barrier faced with wickerwork. The new stretch included a very fast bend and esses (two consecutive bends, a left-hander and a right-hander) which, via the last bend at Tertre Rouge, put the competitors on the road for Mulsanne.

The 24 hours continued to occupy a leading position among European motor races. It had become an event of world-wide interest, attracting the cream of drivers, who homed in on the little town of Sarthe, 135 miles from Paris, once a year. The years followed one another, each bringing further developments in the cars that raced at Le Mans, as the designers strove to overcome the new problems posed by the changing rules of the race.

The race was run for the last time before the Second World War on June 17th and 18th, 1939. Then came the war and the German occupation, during which the circuit was taken over to serve the airport that flanked one side. When the war ended and the will to live revived, France concentrated on getting back on her feet, but there was still time to think about restarting the big race. In 1948 work started on restoring the circuit. The track was still perfect, but everything else had to be rebuilt from scratch as the entire establishment had been razed to the ground. Five new covered grandstands were built, together with big covered terraces, and the pits were redesigned and rebuilt. Bars, restaurants and shops sprung up around the track, and the 'village' of Le Mans was born.

The first postwar 24-hours started on June 25th, 1949, in the presence of the head of state, Vincent Auriol. A crowd of 180 000 watched a new car make its debut: the Ferrari, which has since sped to victory over and over again. The red car, driven by Chinetti and Lord Selsdon, beat the French competition.

In 1955 a tragic episode marred the glorious history of Le Mans and added many names to the roll of those who have died at the track. Levegh's Mercedes collided with Macklin's Austin in front of the main grandstands, rammed into the embankment, spun into the air and exploded, killing its driver and 83 spectators. This was a disaster of gigantic proportions that aroused the fury of the world's press against the race. Faroux, as race director, was criticized because he did not stop the race, but he justified his decision to continue by pointing out that by doing so he had stopped the crowds from swarming round the scene of the accident and hampering rescue operations.

The 1955 tragedy prompted the organizers to review safety measures at the circuit, though these had been steadily improved as the years went by, and the 1956 race was run in July instead of June to give more time for further work on improving safety measures to be completed. Major projects included setting the pits further back from the track to enable the finishing straight to be widened; moving spectator enclosures further back from the track and erecting safety barriers of various types in front of them to protect spectators against any eventuality; the building of two subways, one for pedestrians and the other for cars; and the reconstruction of the refuelling installations in the pits. Detail modifications were made to the track itself, reducing its length by 34 yards to 14 721 yards. Another innovation at Le Mans was the creation of a small 4 836-yard circuit, using the pits area and the finishing straight. It was dedicated to Ettore Bugatti, and, with work completed in April 1965, the French Grand Prix was run on it in 1967. During the years 1971–2 the organizers of the 24-hours decided to eliminate as far as possible the use of public roads as part of the course, and though work has now slowed down somewhat, the first stages in the restructuring of the circuit were completed in a very short time. The principal changes were in the Arnage and White House areas, where a rather narrow piece of road was replaced by a wider one offering improved visibility. This gave 1 400 yards of widened track, to which were added a further 2 205 yards around the esses at White House, and that section of the old track was closed down. At the same time the opportunity was taken to carry out a further programme of works intended to maximize driver safety.

The 24 Hours of Le Mans, as the name suggests, lasts a whole day, and the spectators therefore live there for a day and night. The famous clock, middle right, hangs outside the race control centre.

The flags of the participating
nations and a military band
parade in front of the crowds
before the start. The spectators
abandon the village and take
their places in the stands.

The race has begun. The early
stages are followed with close
attention—the car that leads at
the end of the first lap
receives a long ovation, even
though the finish is over 3 000
miles off. Then attention
wanders: food and drink beckon.
Newsboys sell the 'latest news'.

Though the public loses interest as the hours roll by, the competitors get not a moment's respite. Activity in the pits is as frantic as ever, and the driver's life is not always easy. The competitor in the picture on the right, already stressed by hours at the wheel, has to contend with digging his car out of the sand after leaving the road. Nobody is allowed to help him, for the rules dictate that he must dig it out alone. His equipment aboard the car includes a small shovel, indispensable in moments like this.

Night falls. The village lights up, and the cars' headlamps pierce the darkness on the track. Some who are spending the night at the track huddle in their sleeping bags. At daybreak there's a rush for the cafés, and then it's back to normal—selling souvenirs, playing bowls—while the cars roar on at 120 mph and the pit crews worry. For them, time drags by intolerably slowly.

The race is drawing to a close and the crowds regather. On the giant scoreboard the red crosses tell the sad story of the cars that have dropped out. Soon the rituals of victory will be enacted once more.

François Cevert

A lap at Le Mans

Le Mans is a circuit I really don't like very much, in fact I'm not very keen on the 24 Hour race because it is an event for cars which are not built to last 24 hours. The track itself is not particularly good because there is a three-mile straight—which is silly I think, especially when you consider that slower circuits often produce great racing.

So we start a flying lap. In front of the pits we are in fourth gear, which in the 1973 Matra was something like 10 000 revs, and we hold this until the Dunlop bridge. This righ -hander is no problem—with modern road-holding it's full throttle all the way up—but coming out of the corner there are two jumps, so it is important to make sure that the car is pointing straight ahead. As soon as you've done the second jump you put your foot on the brake, go down to third gear and set the car up for the esses. The esses are very nice to go through, in fact, because

the road is banked a little on each corner and the car seems to go through the right-hander by itself, feeling rather light. We come out of the esses in third gear and stay in third until the sharp right-hander, which is called Tertre Rouge. This corner is taken in second gear and provides no problem. Cars always seem to be running very wide out of this corner because there is a white line painted on the road a few feet in from the edge of the track, and naturally we use all the available tarmac. Even if you're not going fast it's easier on the car to use as much road as possible.

Then comes the big bore. Third gear, fourth gear and we're into fifth about one-third of the way along the straight. Then there is something like $1\frac{1}{2}$ minutes of full-speed, full-throttle, weaving-through-the-mobile-chicane motoring, and it is quite dangerous. Driving at night doesn't really pose any problems because there are reflective signs all the way down the

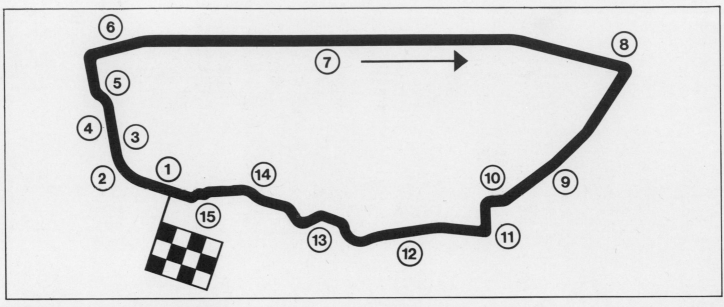

1 The finishing straight runs alongside the pits (protected by a low wall) on the right and past the big grandstands on the outside.

2 At the end of the straight there is a wide curve, which is taken flat out in 4th, while keeping as close to the inside as possible.

3 A slight gradient leads to the Dunlop bridge, where the drivers drop a gear and brake for the esses.

4 The short straight before the esses has two little 'hops' in its surface. Drivers have to be careful not to let their cars be deflected by these.

5 The two bends that make up the esses are very well designed, with the result that they do not represent a difficulty for the drivers, who at this point are in 3rd.

6 This is the short stretch just after Tertre Rouge, and leads into the very long Mulsanne straight, the most boring section.

7 For five km the drivers hurtle along in 5th, with accelerators pressed to the floor. The fastest easily top 180 mph on this stretch.

8 At the end of the long straight comes Mulsanne corner, which has the drivers going down through the gears to 1st, which is engaged just about here.

9 Even on this short straight the fastest cars top the 180 mph mark.

10 Going into the first of the two consecutive bends. The first is called Indianapolis by the drivers and is considered fairly fast, being taken in 3rd.

11 The second bend, called Arnage, is much slower than the first and has the drivers in 1st gear.

12 Accelerating hard and changing up through the box from 1st to 4th, the drivers approach the new part of the circuit, constructed for the 1973 24 Hours.

13 The new stretch begins with a fast right-hander followed by a left-hander. The drivers try to approach these on the right.

14 The last stretch before the grandstand straight is very busy, with a series of narrow bends, each slowing the cars up more than the one before.

15 Before the grandstand straight there is one last difficulty, the very slow Ford chicane, which is taken in 1st.

straight and it is fairly easy to see where you're going. Near the end of the straight there is a flat-out right-hand corner which is really no problem provided you are on the right line, and most people are able to do that. Before the braking area for the Mulsanne corner there is a small hump, on which the car feels very light, and as soon as you come down you put your foot on the brake. During the 24 hour race I lift off at the 400 metres mark, but of course it is possible to brake after the 300 metre mark if you are really trying, and not worrying about conserving the brakes. So I brake at 400 metres, and go down every gear, using the gearbox to help the brakes. I take the Mulsanne corner in first gear and then accelerate back through the gears up to fifth past the signalling pits. This short straight (short in comparison with the Mulsanne straight) is very fast, and we almost reach the same speed as on the Mulsanne—9 500 rpm.

I go into third gear for Indianapolis, a fairly fast right-hander. You must make sure you do not slide too far to the left of the road because then follows a tight left-hander, which I take in second. This is taken at just over 60 mph. Then we come to Arnage, a very slow first gear corner which is no problem at all. Then we accelerate into second, third and fourth, just getting to the rev limiter in fourth before going down to third for the new section of track. This begins with a right-hander, quite fast, and then a left-hander, for which it is again necessary to keep to the right of the track. Still in third gear we come to a very long right-hand corner, where the problem is to stay with the apex all the way round. This is followed by quite a tight left-hander, which is cambered the wrong way and so is taken at low revs in third. Then we accelerate into fourth, go through some fast esses which are quite nice and then brake for two successive chicanes. The first one is second gear—it is a left–right chicane—and the second one, the 'Ford' chicane, is slower and is taken in first gear. Then we start a new lap, accelerating into second, third and fourth.

François Cévert began his racing career in the minor categories, later taking part in some Trophy of France Formula Two races in 1968. In those days he was best known as 'Beltoise's brother-in-law'. Taken on by Tyrrell in 1970, Cévert began to make his own name, showing himself to be a first-rate Formula 1 driver. He was killed in practice for the 1973 American Grand Prix at Watkins Glen.

Monaco

Motor racing writers and journalists have applied hundreds of names—like 'the circuit in the city'—to the circuit that winds around the streets of Monte Carlo, and there can be no doubt that the Monaco Grand Prix is sufficiently extraordinary to justify the wildest flights of journalistic fancy.

The track's 3 584 yards snake through the legendary town, famous as the erstwhile haunt of the noble and very rich, of the great singers of the Café Chantant, of Hollywood stars and industrial barons; famous too for the vast fortunes that have dissolved on the gaming tables of the Casino and for its port that once used to shelter high society's glittering yachts.

With the passing of the years the 'liberty' style of architecture that once predominated in the city's streets has given place to the starkness of reinforced concrete tower blocks. The change has been a violent one, and many are those who mourn the Monte Carlo that was, when in the foyer of the Hôtel de Paris one could meet a cousin of the Tsar, or the Prince of Wales, or La Belle Otero.

It was in 1928 that the idea of disturbing the peace of the Principality with the roar of motors came to Antony Noghès, a wealthy cigarette manufacturer living in Monaco, who was president of the Automobile Club and a good friend of Prince Louis II. Many motives had prompted him to conceive his plan for an automobile race in the city: tourism would undoubtedly benefit, the principality's name would be plastered all over the world's newspapers, and Monte Carlo would thus re-affirm her identity as distinct from France. After a series of discussions with the prince, Noghès's ambitious plan was approved. The experts of the Monaco Automobile Club, under the direct supervision of Noghès, planned the course, and before much time had elapsed the project was ready to be launched. It had already been decided that the first Grand Prix should be run on April 14th, 1929, and all arrangements had to be completed at top speed. The choice of date had been carefully made: between March and May the influx of tourists generally slackened off, and the race would serve as a counter-measure to this. Tourism in those days, of course, was the privilege of the élite, of those who came to Monte Carlo with a Rolls-Royce and a chauffeur.

The course eventually chosen started from the Boulevard Albert I, a road facing the port lined by a row of palatial residences. It curved gently to the right as far as the first bend, known as 'Ste. Dévote' because at that point the road passed by the church of Ste. Dévote, protectress of the principality. It then rose to about 130 feet above sea level up a quite steep hill flanked by big hotels and leading to the Place du Casino. Passing between the Hôtel de Paris and the Casino, and running alongside the pavement in front of the fashion shops and jewellers, the cars then dipped down towards the imposing edifice of the Hôtel Mirabeau. A sharp right-hander and then— still going downhill—they arrived at the Station hairpin, which took them round and practically underneath the Mirabeau; one more corner and they came out on the promenade after passing beneath the arches of the railway bridge. From now on the sea was always in sight, except on the stretch that went through a tunnel called the 'Tir aux Pigeons'; after descending back to sea level, the competitors left the Boulevard Louis II to join the Quai des États-Unis via a chicane. At this stage the cars were actually at the waterside, for on the left of the Quai des États-Unis were bollards and big iron rings for tying up yachts.

Here the circuit planned by Noghès's team came up to a left-hand bend with a tobacconist's shop on the right of the apex, then entered the Quai Albert I, which runs in the opposite direction to the starting straight. A final, difficult hairpin completed the circuit. It was called Gasometer Corner because of the gas works nearby.

When the plan of the projected course was made public there was no lack of protests from shopkeepers whose business would be curtailed by the closing of certain streets, a measure which had to be taken to minimize the element of danger. Yet the combination of a special compensatory payment and appreciation of the community's interests soon produced acquiescence. The idea of the race pleased practically all of Monte Carlo's townspeople, who were not slow to appreciate its possible benefits in terms of tourism, so Noghès had plenty to be pleased about.

Until 1973 the circuit was hardly changed, though with the passing of time a number of the buildings that gave their names to particular corners have been demolished. The old station, for example, is no more, the Mirabeau has gone, and the old pigeon-shooting gallery has been replaced by a gigantic new hotel complex. Times have changed, but the circuit with its traditional names lives on.

However, spurred by the advocates of increased safety, some things have altered. Incredibly enough, and happily, the Monaco circuit has seen few fatal accidents. In the history of the Grand Prix, a great number of accidents have taken place—by its very nature the circuit leaves little margin for error—but in the great majority of cases there has been neither blood spilt nor loss of life. Experts say that this is probably due to the comparatively low speeds that the circuit permits. Indeed it is hard to countenance what could happen if two single-seaters collided at 125 mph on the Boulevard Albert I while hurtling past only a few feet from the packed grandstands. And to think that according to the latest regulations the public should be kept tens of yards back from the edge of the track with a pull-off area, guard rails and safety nets between them and the cars! Evidently Ste. Dévote has always had a soft spot for the race.

Only on five occasions has Monaco's big day ended tragically: when Fagioli had a terrible accident (dying 15 days later), when Lorenzo Bandini was horrifyingly trapped in his blazing red Ferrari (he too died, a few days after), when the Englishman Dennis Taylor and the motorcyclist Norman Lincar lost their lives (during the first and only motorcycle Grand Prix run at Monaco), and when a track marshal was killed, his head struck by a wheel that had come off.

Twice in the history of the Monaco Grand Prix a particularly spectacular accident has occurred—cars have plunged into the sea. This happened to Alberto Ascari in 1955 and ten years later to Paul Hawkins. In both cases the rescue services specifically detailed for this eventuality acted fast, and neither driver suffered serious injury. The stretch of water off the Quai des États-Unis is in fact constantly patrolled during practice and the race itself by a boat with a team of frogmen on board, as well as by a large pontoon equipped with a crane for rapid recovery of the cars. It was these that fished both Ascari and Hawkins out of the water. The idea of patrolling this stretch occurred to the organizers many years ago when the local ace Louis Chiron nearly ended up in the water after a spine-chilling skid.

There has always been a lot of talk and head-shaking about the safety of the Monaco circuit and everyone has voiced their opinion. Among the best qualified voices heard was that of Jackie Stewart, who, as a member of the Grand Prix Drivers' Association, has waged an unremitting campaign for increased safety for his fellow members. 'This is one of the most compelling

circuits, and I like it because it is different from all the others and also because the organizers have really done a lot to make it safe. The changes made after the death of poor Bandini were not called for by the GPDA, and they were carried out immediately, for the organizers knew quite well that they would not be able to justify their position if there was another accident in the place. Some say there are too many guard rails; perhaps there are, but it's much better to be protected by these barriers than to end up against a lamp post, a tree, in a shop window or in among the public. At least I think so.'

Be that as it may, the first major changes to the circuit were made between the 1972 and 1973 Grands Prix. First of all the pits were transferred from the Boulevard Albert I (where they were located under the trees, between the two straights linked by the Gasworks hairpin) to the promenade on the Quai Kennedy, parallel to the Quai des États-Unis. This step was taken in 1972 in answer to a request by the GPDA, who rightly maintained that the pits were in too dangerous a position, and lacked protection where they were. This experiment lasted only one year, for major works were carried out in the winter of 1972–3 and were completed in time for the 1973 Grand Prix. To the existing 3 439 yards of track a further 145 were added (giving a current total of 3 584 yards) by building a new stretch of road leading from the Burea de Tabac bend to the Stade Nautique, going around the swimming pool and then along the edge of the port, and finally rejoining the old road by the Gasworks hairpin after making a tight U-turn around the Restaurant Rascasse. This modification made it possible to restore the pits to their former position in the middle of the Boulevard Albert I, while offering the opportunity of using the Quai Albert I as the pits area and thus keeping them quite separate from the finishing straight. One now enters a pit road at the old Gasometer Corner and leaves more or less by the Automobile Club Monaco office. This and other changes have brought the Monaco circuit into line with the safety stipulations laid down by the FIA, who insist on the pits being isolated from the track. One other change, though brought about for quite different reasons, was the demolition of the 107-yard Tir aux Pigeons tunnel, which has been replaced by a 434-yard gallery beneath a new hotel complex.

Thus safety at Monaco has taken a big step forward. The organizers have once again shown themselves to be far-sighted men, for while spending large sums on the work of modernization in the name of tourism, they have laid firm foundations for the future of the Grand Prix, and for years to come the narrow, picturesque streets of the principality will echo to the sound of racing engines.

Monte Carlo, with its skyscrapers and its harbour filled with the yachts of the rich, offers a colourful setting for the Grand Prix. For four days every year the Formula One stars and the dedicated newcomers in Formula Three race around its streets, while in winter it is the destination of the Monte Carlo rally. On race days there is a special atmosphere—even in the bars, the traditional retreat when the cars are shut up for the night.

Opposite; a view of the port just before the race. All vantage points are crowded with people, the best positions having been occupied since dawn. Above, the bar behind the press stand. Right; yachts bring out the bunting to greet the racers. Below left; a view from above of the swimming-pool area, with the new stretch of track used by cars heading for the pits. Below right; James Hunt, driver for the Hesketh Racing team, with a girl prominently displaying the team's badges.

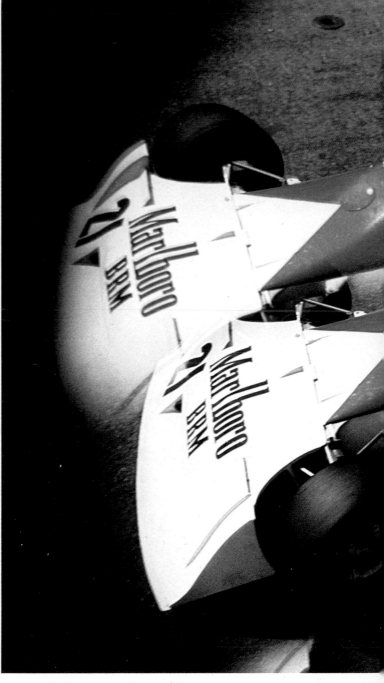

Top left; the helicopter of Radiotélévision Française, based near the swimming-pool. Televised accounts of the Grand Prix have always been good, particularly the shots taken from the air. Left; a mini-publicity parade, featuring pretty girls. Right; the corner which has replaced the famous Gasometer bend. It is called La Rascasse, the name of the restaurant it turns around. Here one may lunch while watching the race—a rather special feature.

Left; Denny Hulme, veteran of the McLaren team, in conversation with one of his crew during practice. Below left; the McLaren cars again, waiting to move out on to the starting grid. Below right; a car in the pits, the centre of attention.

Right; the big illuminated arrows placed at the pits exit to safeguard drivers and marshals. Far right; a marshal safe inside the guard-rail as Peter Revson's McLaren speeds by. Below; François Cevert solves an age-old problem. Bottom; Carlos Reutemann waits in the pits for practice to start. Right; the new stretch around the swimming-pool, with Jackie Ickx leading in a Ferrari.

Crowds everywhere. The nearness of the cars, the smells of petrol, oil and tormented tyres—all these produce a truly thrilling atmosphere, almost unique to Monaco. Perhaps spectators are at greater risk here, but the race's attraction is stronger than the fear of injury.

Graham Hill

A lap at Monaco

From the start/finish line, which is on the town side of the pits, the road starts to climb to St Devote, which is one of the fastest corners on the circuit, about 95 mph. I take the corner in third gear and come out at about 9 000 rpm. You start lifting well before the corner and you've just got to clip the curb on the apex to get it right, then out as far as the barriers on the left to exit at the fastest possible speed. You give the car full acceleration up the steep hill towards the Casino Square: about half way up you change into fourth and there's a little bit of a swerve in the middle of the hill that you try to straighten out.

You come over the crest of the hill, and it is important to get your braking just right for this point, because if you leave it a little bit too late over the top of that hill, the car gets very light and you lock the back wheels up and get right out of control. So it is very important to get off the throttle correctly and just *ease* on the brakes to start with, so the car is then steady for the approach to the left-hander. I drop into third for this corner, and it pays to hug the kerb as much as possible, because the road itself is rather heavily cambered in both directions. I try to put the inside wheels right in next to the gutter and make use of my side of the camber.

I just clip the kerb outside the Hotel de Paris, then get off the throttle, give a quick flick to the right and put the car into a bit of a drift to go round Casino Square in third gear. This gear is normally a little bit high for this corner because you have a toss-up whether to get it right for Ste Devote or for this one. You can't have it exactly correct for both. Anyway, I choose to have it a little high for the Square, that's why I chuck the car into the corner and promote a drift, then give it a bootfull of throttle again as I go over the hump by the gardens. The cars get very light here

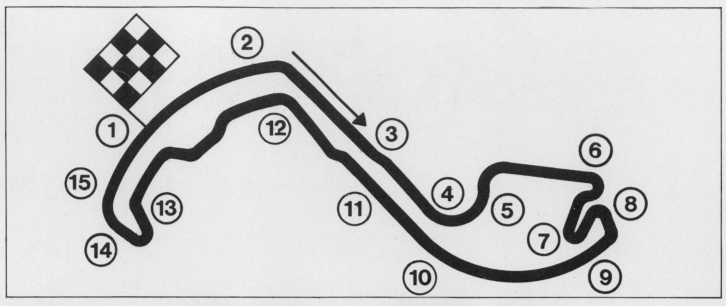

1 The finishing straight, into which the pits exit opens.

2 Having passed the pits exit, the drivers prepare to take the Ste Dévote bend, which leads to the uphill stretch.

3 The straight that goes towards the Hôtel de Paris takes the drivers from sea level to the Casino square.

4 Before the square is reached there is a relatively fast bend, protected on both sides by guard rails. The famous Casino can be seen in the background.

5 The entrance to the square is in the form of a kind of esses, with the pavement in front of the Hôtel de Paris on one side and the central roundabout on the other.

6 After a short downhill straight one arrives at Mirabeau corner, and here the most tortuous stretch of the circuit begins.

7 The famous Station hairpin, still thus called although the station has given place to yet another skyscraper.

8 Leaving Station hairpin, the drivers take the two further bends that lead them down to the promenade.

9 The entrance to the new tunnel, which comes much earlier than the entrance to the old Tir Aux Pigeons.

10 The covered section is long and curving. Above it is a new hotel complex, replacing the Tir aux Pigeons.

11 Continuing the descent that leads down to sea level, one reaches the chicane leading on to the mole.

12 The Tabac bend was widened in 1973. It marks the beginning of the entirely new stretch of the Monaco circuit, rebuilt for safety reasons.

13 Having taken two narrow bends with a short straight between them, one heads for the La Rascasse corner.

14 Coming out of the sharp right-hander, one passes the place where the Gasometer that gave its name to a famous corner once stood. The road ascends slightly here.

15 One completes the lap by coming back on to the finishing straight. The pits entrance is here.

and often you'll see photos of cars with the wheels off the ground. This causes them to move across the road towards the barrier on the outside.

After the Square it's a short, sharp acceleration down the road—quite a hill—past the night clubs, the Tip Top and so on. Then you brake quite heavily for Mirabeau, a second gear corner.

Then I give a good heavy boot in second gear down towards the Station Hairpin—the tail slides out and you make sure you don't hit the kerb on the left—and then flick it left again down into the hairpin. The Station is no longer there but we still call it the Station Hairpin. This is a first gear corner and you brake hard. The front wheels normally tend to lock up here because you get heavy braking from the engine at this point, while in second gear. Then you drop it into first and let it *run* round the hairpin. If you put the power on too early you'll push the front out and this will make you understeer into the straw bales and give you the wrong line for the next corner. *Just* at the right moment you need to feed the throttle in, get the tail out a little bit and change up into second for the right-hander that leads you down to the sea front.

We go on under the railway bridge to the sea front, again in second gear, and drift out to the sea wall, again clipping the kerb on the inside. Then I try to get off the pavement as soon as I can and back on to the road to miss one or two of the bumps, and thus try to relieve the load on the transmission, which always gets a hell of a pasting at Monte Carlo. Then I change into third, fourth and just snick it into fifth before I go into the tunnel.

The tunnel is right in the middle of a corner, so the apex is inside the tunnel, and you want to clip the kerb there—which is difficult. They do put lights in the tunnel, but the sudden entry from bright sunshine into comparative darkness means that the eye is just not quite quick enough in changing, so you do have a bit of trouble in seeing the kerb and getting the position of the car just right.

Of course, you come hurtling out into the bright light again and just about have time to get up to maximum revs in top gear—this is the fastest part of the circuit. The road runs uphill a bit and at the crest you back off, the car gets very light. You start braking very gently at first, and then more heavily as you approach the chicane—which always seems terribly narrow—give it a quick flick to left and then right, and out on to the waterfront, the side of the harbour.

Just before the old Tobacconists' Corner the circuit now turns left on to a new 'Mickey Mouse' section round the swimming pool. The initial, fairly fast, left-hander is followed by a short straight, a tight left–right ess-bend, another short straight, a right–left ess and then a left hand curve which leads into the right hand hairpin round the Rascasse Restaurant. In the old days it was possible to pass other cars on the run down from the Tobacconists to the Gasworks Hairpin; this is completely impossible on the new section, and to make matters worse there is a big bump where it rejoins the old one. The one good thing about it is that the pits are now completely separate from the track, with ample room to work on the cars and with quite good entry and exit points.

Graham Hill

Graham Hill, a Londoner born on February 15th, 1929, is the grand old man of Formula One racing. He entered the racing scene in 1954 as a mechanic, gradually rising to be world champion. He has driven in a tremendous number of races and has a fine record of successes, including five wins in the Monaco GP, two world championship titles, and a win at Indianapolis and Le Mans.

Monza

When the wounds of the First World War began to heal, the Italian motor industry expressed the view that motor sporting successes were needed to stimulate Italian exports of motor cars. A need was felt not only to build new and more powerful racing cars but also to create a major racetrack on which these cars could show their paces.

Thus the idea was born of building a modern, permanent and enclosed racing circuit, with lots of room for the public and with all subsidiary services. Leading protagonists were the senators Silvio Crespi and Arturo Mercanti, respectively president and director of the Automobile Club Milano in the 1920s.

Having rejected a proposal to build a circuit in the area of Gallarate and another that favoured La Cagnola (near Milan) as the ideal location, the heads of the Automobile Club Milano were impressed by the suggestion that the circuit should be built at Monza, in the Park adjoining the royal villa. This solution seemed ideal, and a company was formed to develop the project, the SIAS (Società Incremento Autodromo e Sport) with fully paid-up capital, under the presidency of Silvio Crespi. Agreements were then concluded with the Opera Nazionale Combattente (who administered the Park) and with the Consorzio Milano-Monza, and the planning of the project was entrusted to the Impresa Piero Puricelli. Preliminary cost forecasts indicated that 16 million lire would be needed to lay a speed track and a 'road' circuit, combined in such a way that they could be used simultaneously or separately, with a total extent of 8·69 miles.

The first sod was turned by Vincenzo Lancia and Felice Nazzaro in an elaborate inaugural ceremony on February 26th, 1922, but only a few days later the work was to be halted on the grounds that the project was detrimental to the aesthetic value of the site and to the conservation of the countryside. Protests came thick and fast from the motor industry and motor sport enthusiasts, and eventually Rome gave its permission for work to be resumed, although it was soon discovered that the conditions imposed were such as radically to alter the original plan.

'We'll have the circuit ready for the Grand Prix of Italy,' the heads of the SIAS had that year affirmed, and they now had only five months left. The architects succeeded in redesigning the parts of the project that had met with ministerial displeasure, and soon the new plans were approved. But time was pressing. 3 500 workmen were employed, along with 200 wagons, 300 lorries and even a small Decauville railway three miles long. Two locomotives and 80 wagons were in constant use on the mini-railway set up among the trees of the park.

In 110 days the entire complex was finished. Besides the track there were pits, grandstands and service roads. On August 20th, three Fiats, driven in turn by Nazzaro, Bordino, Salamano, Giaccone and Lampiano drove round the 4 921-yard speed circuit, which was made up of two 1 094-yard straights linked by two curves with an average radius of 350 yards. Then they tried the 6 015-yard 'road' circuit, which included a number of varied bends as well as two straights. The two circuits crossed via a tunnel on the North bend, and the straight that ran in front of the grandstands, 26·2 yards wide, was common to both circuits. The track surface was a concrete mixture of cement and fine calcareous gravel, while the road circuit was rolled with tarred gravel. The entire track measured 6·21 miles.

On August 28th, 1922, the track was opened with a colourful ceremony. Two hundred members of the Automobile Club Milano filed round the circuit in their cars before the competitors started practice for the Voiturette GP and for the GP of Italy, both to take place on September 3rd. The first years went by, with safety always in the minds of the track's organizers. Further measures were taken to protect the public, including earthen banks and metal safety nets.

On September 9th, 1928, on the occasion of the eighth Italian Grand Prix, all these protective measures proved to be of no avail. As the cars roared past the grandstands for the eighteenth time Materassi's Talbot, which was just overtaking Foresti's Bugatti, swerved suddenly to the left—nobody yet knows why. The Talbot crashed through the barriers and into the spectators before falling, silent into the ditch. Materassi was killed immediately and the car mowed down many spectators, the toll being 27 dead and 21 injured.

Accidents are the least happy part of the history of a circuit, but because of the strong emotions they arouse they naturally enough stay longest in the memory and are often the cause of radical modifications to the very shape of a circuit. Thus it was after the tragedy of the 1928 Italian GP: as a direct consequence of it, major steps were taken to afford the public a greater degree of safety. Advances in technology can also necessitate modernization. Thus at Monza in 1930 work was put in hand on a 328-yard link between the central straight and the east straight of the speed circuit, which cut out the banked North curve and the Vedano bend of the road circuit, both in bad repair. The track thus created was 7 503 yards long and was named the Florio circuit.

The second accident that involved the public happened the following year, on September 6th, 1931. Philippe Etancelin in an Alfa Romeo left the road at Lesmo and ploughed into a group of spectators; three people died, including Etancelin, and fourteen were injured. This time there was only an inquest into the mechanics of the accident and no guilt was attributed to the circuit.

1933 on the other hand was a year that the 'defenders' of Monza were not able to forget so quickly. The day's racing on October 10th saw the deaths of no fewer than three great drivers: on the South curve of the speed circuit Giuseppe Campari's P3 Alfa Romeo and Baconin Borzacchini's 8CM Maserati slid on a large patch of oil spilt by the Scuderia Ferrari's 4·5 litre

Duesenberg; completely out of control, the cars became the two luckless champions' iron coffins. Count Stanislas Czaykowski's fate was also sealed. In the final moments of that same Monza Grand Prix, which was being contested on the same day as the Italian Grand Prix, the Polish driver lost control of his big Bugatti while tackling the dreaded South curve; the car turned over and burst into flames. The track became the scapegoat for this triple tragedy, and for many years no races were run on the old 6·21-mile circuit and the 4 921-yard speed circuit.

In 1938 an engineer called Aldo di Rionzo drafted a programme of radical renovations, including not only the rebuilding of the circuit but also the modernization of the auxiliary installations. The new track tended to allow a wider range of speeds—very high speeds on the straights but severe reductions on speeds in the bends. In practice the operation meant abandoning and demolishing the speed circuit, the old central straight and the lesser South curve; building a new central straight 2 253 yards long to the west of the old one and parallel to the grandstand straight, linked to the old stretch leaving the Lesmo curves via the new Vialone curve. In addition, the grandstand straight was extended to 1 957 yards, being linked to the new central straight by two short transverse straights and four flat bends, three with a 65·6-yard radius and the fourth with a 218·7-yard radius. The

track would have a minimum width of 9·8 yards and a maximum of 13·1.

The work was carried out in two stages. Started in 1938, when the Italian Grand Prix was run on the old circuit, it was completed in 1939–40. The new circuit was used with some slight modifications until 1955, the year in which it was decided to build a new speed circuit with banked curves.

But before 1955 two more dramatic incidents were added to the circuit's annals. In 1952 Fangio—one of the greatest racing drivers of all time—was nearly killed when he left the track at Lesmo. A more tragic event took place during tests on May 26th, 1955. Alberto Ascari, who had survived plunging into the sea during the Monaco Grand Prix a few days earlier, saw Castellotti lapping in a new Ferrari sports car and pleaded with his friend to let him have a turn at the wheel: he didn't even get a quarter of the way round the circuit. His friends Villoresi and Castellotti found him dead on the grass just beyond the Vialone bend with the wrecked car beside him.

The changes made to the circuit in 1955 were extensive, restoring the two great banked curves to their former glory, resting on a concrete structure. The existing circuit was reduced from 6 889 to 6 288 yards, and the new Indianapolis-type bowl roughly followed the one that had been built long ago, in 1922. The two circuits—speed and road—could be used simultaneously, with a total extent of 6·21 miles and a grandstand straight used by both.

The layout of the circuits has remained the same since 1955, although in 1959 the SIAS decided to create a new, shorter circuit specially for the new smaller cars; this 'Pista Junior' is 3 100 yards long and was made by linking the grandstand straight with the one opposite.

1961 brought tragedy to Monza once again. During the second lap of the 32nd Italian Grand Prix, Clark and von Trips collided in the braking area for the Parabolica. The German's Ferrari hit the outer bank, which threw it into the air. The car turned over and twice hit the net holding the public in before crashing back on to the track. This accident exacted a heavy toll: von Trips and ten spectators lost their lives, while of the fifteen taken to hospital there were five for whom nothing could be done.

The death of these fifteen spectators caused an intensive and violent Press campaign against motor racing in general and against Monza in particular. After carrying out a series of studies, the SIAS decided to adopt various measures designed to offer better safety precautions for the public.

Since this disaster no more spectators have been involved in accidents at the track, though these continue to happen. Other drivers have lost their lives: the promising Bruno Deserti, the Swiss Tommy Spychiger, the Englishman Boley Pittard and, in 1970, the Austrian Jochen Rindt.

Meanwhile no substantial modifications have been made to the circuit, apart from the chicanes sited at the end of the pits straight and in the Vialone curve, which have increased the length of the track by 109 yards.

One of the problems facing the organizers of the Italian GP every year is that of controlling the public. The pits for instance are an irresistible attraction and spectators are continually trying to get over or through the fences that surrounds them. Monza attracts young and old, men and women alike. Souvenir sellers do good business. Young people take the opportunity to lounge on the grass before practice begins.

A moment long awaited: the Ferraris arrive, and enthusiasts stand by ready to help. The Ferrari transporter displays its destination on the front (far left). Also left; three lovelies in the pits; the nearest is Mrs Fittipaldi, wife of the Brazilian 1973 world champion. Top right; the flags of the nations represented. Right; getting ready for official practice in the Ferrari pit.

137

Left; Emerson Fittipaldi's black and gold JPS being tended by its black-clad mechanics in front of the garages. Below left; Denis Hulme adjusting his McLaren's wing before practice. Below right; a Surtees in the pits being pored over by its crew. Opposite page, top; tyre marks at the exit of Ascari bend testify to the trickiness of this part of the circuit. Centre; an aerial view of the Parabolica, with the cars in Indian file. Bottom; Hulme's McLaren leads Lauda's March, with Mike Beuttler's privately entered March further behind. The rubber cones mark off the artificial chicane used in the 1972 Italian Grand Prix. Far right; a huge hoarding converted into a rather insecure grandstand.

Two views of Monza's
ever-enthusiastic spectators.
Those in the picture on the left
display a wide variety of
reactions to the car they are
watching, from thumbs-up to
thumbs-down, with a few
whistles to boot.

Andrea de Adamich

A lap at Monza

Monza was once thought of as one of the fastest and least selective of all circuits, especially for single seaters, because it was possible to get a 'tow' in the slipstream of another car round the whole lap. With the aid of this tow, slower cars could exceed their normal 'solo' maximum speed. The useful slipstream of the fastest cars extended as far as 200 yards behind them, and cars with less powerful engines were sucked along in this natural vent. Thus, provided the tow was not broken, cars with less powerful engines could equal the fastest in speed.

A slipstreaming driver could gain on a nominally faster leading car. For example, if a single-seater driver managed to trail a faster car out of the Parabolica (a good exit from this corner was essential), he could then progressively gain the speed of the 'towing' car, and build up such a speed advantage that he could 'catapult' out of the slipstream and overtake the

faster car as they came up to the pits. On the old Monza circuit, therefore, the driver wasn't required to perform the impossible. One built up to maximum speed in fifth gear along the main straight and held it round the Curva Grande, then dropped to fourth then third to tackle the two Lesmo corners, went up through fourth to fifth through the Ascari bend (or Curva del Vialone). This led into the Rettilineo Centro, and at the end of this straight one started braking at the 200 metre board for the third gear Parabolica. Coming out of the Parabolica one had to accelerate hard through fourth and into fifth gear, using maximum revs to build up speed as quickly as possible for the very fast stretch at the start of the next lap.

However, in 1972 two 'temporary' chicanes were built, expressly to break up the slipstreaming groups of cars which some drivers and officials insisted were dangerous. One chicane was at the end of

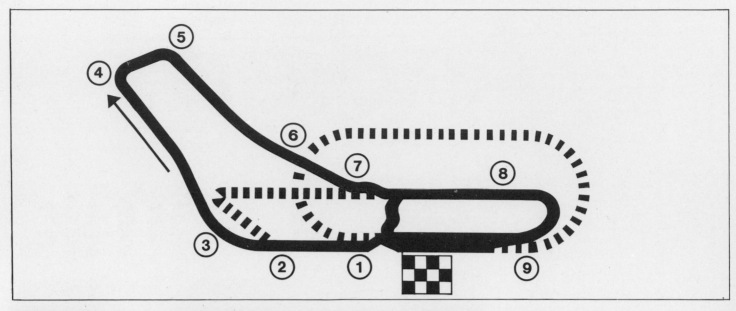

Born in Trieste on October 3rd, 1941, Andrea de Adamich began his racing career in 1961. Six years later he was taken on by Alfa Romeo and went over to Ferrari at the end of 1967. After a nasty accident at Brands Hatch, he stayed out of racing for some months before going back to Alfa Romeo at the end of 1968, winning at Brands Hatch and Watkins Glen for them in 1971. In Formula 1 he has driven McLaren, March, Surtees and Brabham cars.

1 The finishing straight featured this temporary chicane, which forced drivers to reduce speed violently.

2 The straight leading to the Curva Grande. It is on this stretch that single seaters reach their highest speed, after negotiating the chicane erected to stop drivers slipstreaming.

3 The beginning of the Curva Grande which modern formula single seaters take at speeds of 155–170 mph.

4 The first of the two Lesmo bends. The area takes its name from the place just the other side of the circuit's outer wall. Here the cars are in 3rd gear.

5 Leaving the second Lesmo bend, taken in 4th, one sees the Dunlop bridge, built to allow pedestrians to cross the track.

6 After a short, descending straight one reaches the underpass at about 170 mph, crossing beneath the South bend of the old banked track.

7 After the underpass one heads for Ascari bend, where a chicane is sited. Here one reduces speed substantially, dropping from 5th to 3rd.

8 Leaving the chicane, one goes down the straight leading to the difficult Parabolica curve. The driver who brakes last gains the advantage.

9 After the Parabolica is the long grandstand straight, the pits and the finish line. At this point the cars are already in 5th gear.

143

the wide straight past the pits, the other in the Curva del Vialone. These changed the nature of the circuit, and now I pass in front of the pits in fifth gear, without using full power. About a hundred yards past the finishing line I brake very strongly at the 150 metre sign, keeping well over to the right of the usable track. A quick change from fifth straight to third, then down to second, and I steer left–right through the first chicane. The car slides its rear wheels under acceleration in second gear, and I then go up quickly through all gears to fifth, to reach full speed through the Curva Grande.

I brake at the 150 metre marker at the entrance to the first Lesmo corner, change down from fifth to third, then up to fourth for the second Lesmo. I accelerate hard in fourth, and take fifth gear just before the bridge where the old banked track passes over the circuit, working up towards maximum speed on the slight climb to the Vialone. A 200 metre board warns that you are coming to the second chicane, and I start braking. The car must be kept straight, on the right, before turning quickly to the left into the chicane. I enter this in second gear; half way through, the road widens, and I change to third, then to fourth at the exit. The straight leading to the Parabolica allows you to get into fifth gear, but is not long enough for full power to develop. Before the Parabolica I brake, accelerate through the bend in third, change up to fourth, then into fifth to pass the pits at the end of the lap.

The old circuit required only eight gear changes, but the introduction of the two chicanes means that an additional ten changes are needed on each lap.

144

Nürburgring

It has happened that circuits have been created for political reasons, and this was certainly the case as far as Nürburgring was concerned. Although the circuit was not inaugurated until June 18th, 1927, the plan had first been tabled nearly 20 years earlier. The idea for a permanent circuit in the Eifel region had first been discussed in 1907—on the day after Felice Nazzaro had won the Kaiserpreis for Fiat on the Taunus circuit near Frankfurt. The Kaiser, who had hoped for a 'home' win, angrily demanded a precise explanation for this most unexpected defeat. He was told that fault could be attributed entirely to the lack of a circuit suitable for trials and competitions. His brother—a passionate motoring enthusiast—also intervened, lending weight to the persuasive arguments offered by Kaiser Wilhelm II's advisers.

Once the imperial consent had been given, nothing stood in the way. It was merely a matter of getting work started. The choice of site had long since fallen on the region surrounding the town of Adenau, near the Eifel and the castle of Nürburg, an imposing edifice built in 1167, but just as the enthusiasts were beginning to look forward to the day when the circuit would be ready, war intervened and dispelled such frivolous thoughts from their minds. Germany emerged from the war defeated; the currency was valueless, and hardship hit every family. Yet thoughts turned once again to the circuit that was once going to be built near the castle of Nürburg. In 1920 the project was tentatively presented to the authorities, but it foundered because of the impossibility of raising the necessary funds. One man retained a blind and unswerving faith in the idea, and in the opportunities it could offer the resurgent German motor industry for trials and competition. This man, who presented the most compelling arguments in favour of his ideas, was Dr Crentz, President of the ADAC (Allgemeiner Deutscher Automobile Club). Having reached an agreement with the Mayor of Cologne, Konrad Adenauer (who later became Chancellor), Crentz presented the programme of works necessary for the construction of the circuit as a concrete means of reducing unemployment.

The first stone was laid on September 27th, 1925. For two years more than 3 000 workmen laboured to construct the circuit planned by Hans Weidenbruke. It was to wind through the Eifel massif in Renania, not far from Cologne, Bonn, Koblenz and Düsseldorf. There were two circuits:

the North circuit, the one normally used for races, was 14·18 miles long; the South circuit only 4·81 miles long. The two circuits shared the pits area and the main straight. Nürburgring soon became famous for its 176 bends (85 right-handers and 91 left-handers) and because parts of the track climbed to 2 034 feet above sea level, with gradients of up to 17 per cent— the road followed the configuration of the terrain, and there were lots of dips and bumps to test suspensions.

Divided into four 4·5-mile sections, construction work on the entire track cost 15 million marks, but it absorbed a lot of spare manpower and thus fulfilled the promise that Crentz had made when presenting his proposals. Naturally appeals were made to other possible sources of finance by stressing the advantages in terms of an increase in tourism that the presence of the circuit would bring, as well as the technological advances that motor manufacturers might be able to make as a result of testing their machines on this difficult and arduous course. Besides the 6 million marks provided by the government, the vice president of the ADAC received substantial finance from the city of Cologne.

In twenty months construction work was complete on about 100 brick-built pits, a large grandstand with a capacity of 10 000 (a second grandstand was later built nearby), a hotel, a restaurant, the circuit offices, the race control tower, the garages, and a subway giving access to the straight. A few days before the end of September 1927 the Nordschleife was finished (completion of the Sudschleife followed a year later).

Thus Germany's first permanent racing circuit was born, putting her in the same league as Britain with the legendary Brooklands track, Italy with the super-fast Monza circuit, and France with Montlhéry.

The first race was for motorcycles, won by Tony Ulman on a Velocette, and on the next day came the first car race. Rudolf Caracciola was the first man to win a motor race at Nürburgring, in a supercharged Mercedes S. The Grand Prix came to Nürburgring on July 17th, 1927, when the second German Grand Prix was contested, the first having been run on the Arus circuit in the previous year.

Nürburgring was a name chosen by means of a competition, the winning entry coming from a retired government official from Bad Godesberg. The circuit rapidly became popular among both drivers and an ever-growing public. Between 1927 and 1970 it was not substantially modified, though some widening was carried out and improved spectator facilities were provided. The last great pre-war race at the 'Ring' was run on July 23rd, 1939, and saw Rudi Caracciola score his sixth German Grand Prix victory, and his fifth for Mercedes.

After the Second World War, Germany was again in a state of collapse. There was no money about, and with the German people struggling against hardship and deprivation, there was certainly none to be had for rebuilding the circuit. Yet thanks to the enthusiasm of the French who had been given the task of overseeing the area, the Nürburgring was soon back on its feet— events had indeed taken a marvellous though unexpected turn.

On August 17th, 1947, motorcycles racing round the South circuit opened the second great era in the history of the Nürburgring. In one respect this race was a curiosity. It may even have been unique, for the price of a ticket included a meal of two sausages, potato salad, some bread and half a litre of wine. This combination of racing with food and drink was too much for young people to resist, and they flocked to the meeting. There was also the problem of the national flag that was customarily used by the starter of the race—at that particular sensitive time Germany had no flag, and the start was therefore signalled with a white flag.

In 1950 the single-seaters returned, for a Formula 2 event (the first German GP to count as a world championship race was not run until the following year); in 1953 the first 1 000 kilometres, for sports and sports-racing cars, took place; in 1955 the Pokalrennen, for smaller categories of single-seaters, was run. Now the 'Ring' had regained its true international status.

As far as safety is concerned, and considering how difficult the circuit is, the Nürburgring has never claimed great sacrifices of life and limb. It is undoubtedly possible to make a number of mistakes before one knows the track well enough (if anybody does), but such errors and misjudgements have never yet proved fatal. Be that as it may, the organizers of Nürburgring recently had to accede to the requests of the GPDA and the CSI, and a major programme of modernization has been undertaken, including erecting safety barriers, moving the spectators further back from the edge of the course, and organizing a first-rate emergency service.

A day's racing at the Nürburgring has a special fascination. Within its 20·4 miles it can accommodate enormous numbers of people (more than

350 000 for the Grand Prix, it is claimed) and camping is the order of the day. According to a statistical study carried out by the ADAC and the AvD (Automobilclub von Deutschland) about a million people attend races at the Nürburgring in the course of a year. Around 3 500 drivers use the track, and an average of over 150 000 litres of petrol is consumed per race. The village of Nürburg is typical of the region, and each year approximately 12 000 people spend a night there. In twelve months the kiosks around the circuit dispense 300 000 rolls and 600 000 bottles of beer. The economic effects of a racing fixture at the Nürburgring are felt within a radius of 30 miles from Nürburg. An enquiry into the amounts of money the members of the public spend has revealed that 45 per cent of them spend 50 marks each and 30 per cent spend 100.

Tourists come from all over the world to visit the Nürburgring and ride round the circuit amidst the natural beauties of the Eifel region. It has been calculated that every year more than 90 000 cars, almost 20 000 motorcycles and 1 000 coaches lap the circuit. On average the cars have two people on board, the buses forty. Thus one might conclude that the Nürburgring is visited by around 250 000 people every year. Immediately after races the circuit is opened to the public, and it is not unusual to see motorists flying off the road or crashing into trees in a (failed) attempt to imitate the aces whose prowess they have been admiring on the same circuit minutes before.

Among current circuits the Nürburgring is a rather special case: though essentially made up of quite ordinary roads—apart from the track beside the pits, which is 72 feet wide—it offers extensive safety measures, allied to natural difficulties, which make it at one and the same time one of the circuits best loved and one of the most feared by racing drivers. At the Nürburgring, in fact, only the truly great drivers win.

The Nürburgring is set in beautiful countryside, with wooded slopes and verdant meadows. Camping, above and right, is an integral feature of German races, while consumption of beer—taken to extremes by the gentlemen opposite—is spectacularly high during the long hours of waiting. Nürburgring offers an infinite number of natural vantage points to watch the racing from. Opposite bottom; an idyllic scene, with the old castle of Nürburg in the distance.

Left; the tall white tower that houses the race control and other services. Above; the entrance to the pits. Bottom left; the big central grandstand opposite the pits is naturally one of the most sought-after positions, giving the best view of the racing. Below; the inevitable souvenir hawker.

The paddock is behind the pits and is particularly well laid out.
Below; sports cars are an irresistible attraction for the public.
Right; two fire-fighting vehicles.

Above; activity and inactivity in the pits before the start.
Opposite; racing in full swing. The big picture shows the
masterful Jackie Stewart tackling the famous Karussel corner.

After the grandstand straight the competitors come to a particularly testing section. Left; one of the signal towers, giving up-to-the-minute information on positions. Above; the winners: the Ferrari team celebrate a victory. Here are Regazzoni, Ickx (with the cup) and the mechanics.

Jacky Ickx

A lap at the Nürburgring

After the start, the first corner is a left-hander taken in third gear. This is quite a difficult corner because it is relatively fast and you can never really see the end of it. Then you have to run half throttle all the way round the South Curve and only apply full power right at the end of the corner. I then accelerate hard along the straight behind the pits, getting into top gear before the North Curve. I brake for the North Curve when I'm about level with the start/finish line and then take the corner in third gear, going straight from top to third. Immediately after this is a very difficult section, because you jump over a bridge and then turn left as soon as you land—you have to fly with the car and then brake at the right moment to take the left-hander, so I always stay well to the right of the road approaching the jump.

Then there is a very fast flat-out-in-fourth downhill right-hander, a very important corner because you can gain a lot

of time there. The camber of the road is also 'wrong', so it's quite difficult and I use all the road. Then I brake very hard and select third gear for the 'esses' at Hatzenbach and stay in that gear all the way to the straight at Flugplatz. There are four corners in the 'esses', and I straight line through them as much as possible. You have to be very precise through this section.

Next is the right hand corner leading to Flugplatz, a very important corner because there it is followed immediately by a long straight immediately afterwards. Then we go up to fifth gear, staying in top over Flugplatz, where I quickly back off, jump, and then immediately take a very high-speed right-hander. Most drivers take this in fourth, but I think it's easier in fifth. It is followed by a very fast and slightly left hand section down to the next bridge, at Aremberg. Before the bridge there is a downhill positive-camber right-hander,

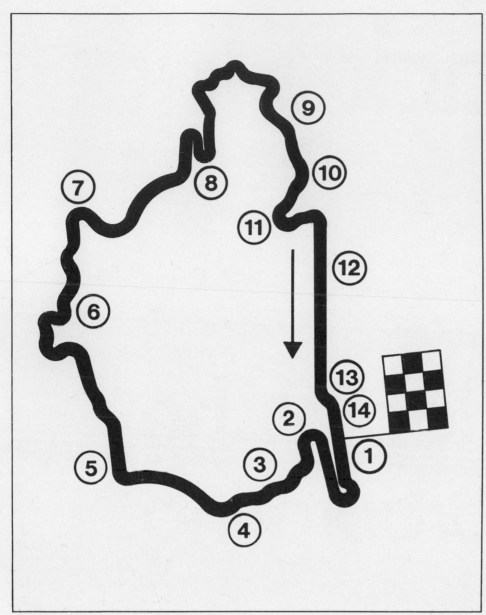

1 The finishing straight leads to a fast left-hander and then to the South bend, which puts the cars on the parallel straight.

5 Immediately after the Arenberg bend one passes under a bridge. At this point most drivers are in 3rd gear.

9 At the seventeenth kilometre one passes through the Pflanzgarten area, another fast section with a lot of bumps.

10 About half a mile later one comes to an elongated esses which forces one to keep to the outside of the first bend, though this is not too difficult.

11 Another bend, the Schwalbenschwanz, looking much like the Karussel. It is taken in 3rd gear.

2 Leaving the North bend one hits a rather tricky section of track. It has bumps and undulations which can result in loss of adhesion.

3 Here the cars momentarily take to the air, launched by an irregularity in the surface that acts as a take-off ramp.

4 In the Flugplatz area there is an important bend, leading to a relatively fast section on which one can use the full power of one's engine.

6 This stretch descends and is known as Fuchsrohre. It is characterized by some very fast blind bends.

7 One arrives at Bergwerk, a right-hander, at very high speed and takes the succeeding bends flat out, without slowing down.

8 This is the entrance to the celebrated Karussel, with the surface banked at two different angles. Drivers keep to the inside of it.

12 After the Dottinghohe corner comes the long undulating straight, which one drives down trying to hold the car in the middle of the road.

13 At the end of the straight there is a bend immediately after a bridge. This is a difficult spot because it is tackled at very high speed.

14 After the esses, which slow the cars right down, one arrives back on the finishing straight, with the pits entrance on the right.

159

which is taken quite fast in third gear. Then there is a very fast downhill section through Fuchsrohre with a series of blind corners which I can take virtually flat-out in fifth gear, sliding from one side of the road to the other. Most cars bottom through there, so this is one of the places that determines the setting of ride height. The g-forces are not too bad, but it is very hard on the suspension.

Then we go up again to the slow right–left–right section at the 7 km post. These are second gear corners, and it is usually very easy to spin here because you can't see the track ahead of you and the left-hander is very tight: it's a place you have to keep as far to the inside as possible as the outside of the road is usually fairly slippery.

A relatively fast straight follows, with a left hand corner at the end for which I go down from fifth to fourth. Then it's down to third for Metzgesfeld, before arriving at the down-hill section leading to Adenau. I take the first right-hander at Adenau in third gear, and as the corner has slight positive camber, it's quite enjoyable. Then there is a very fast section down to Adenau, consisting of three very difficult right-handers.

Then you go down to the first bridge of Adenau, at Wehrseifen—a fast second gear left-hander with two walls either side to make vision difficult. Over the bridge there is a short straight before a big jump at Ex-Muhle. This is followed by a down-hill left-hander which you don't brake for, and you therefore just go from one side of the road to the other. It is very difficult, because there is the same problem as before: you're bottoming and then braking hard for the corner ahead.

Continuing down to Adenau, the jump is followed by a fast left, where it's important to stay very close to the hedge. This is followed by a very quick up-hill right-hander which is taken in third gear. It is followed by a very fast top gear section where I get off the ground two or three times. Then I brake very hard for the right-hander, Bergwerk, which leads on to the very, very fast section before the Karussel.

Then we arrive at the Karussel, a third gear corner. You have to stay very close to the inside because if you slip out of the banking you just go straight off—the top of the road is just flat. You can really feel the g-forces through the Karussel, and I keep the throttle in a constant half-open position. As soon as I can see the outside of the corner I put the power on. The car slides a little bit coming out, but it's no real problem.

The Karussel is followed by another fast section leading to the 15 km. post, the highest point of the circuit. This is taken in fourth gear and is a place where it is relatively easy to spin because the road is usually quite slippery (I don't know why, but it is more slippery there than in any other place). The road then goes to the left and right, up and down, and finally comes to a place called Brunnchen, where until 1970 there was a very high jump. Now they have cut the jump completely, but it is still quite difficult, because this is always a place where there is shadow on the road due to the surrounding trees.

Then we arrive at another fast section, Pflanzgarten, which I run in top gear, and where, as with all the fast sections of the Nürburgring, there are a lot of jumps. This is then followed by Dottinger Höhe, a corner that looks like the Karussel, and is also taken in third.

Dottinger Höhe leads on to the main straight at the end of which there is a left corner under the bridge, a very difficult corner which I take almost flat. Then we arrive at the esses before the pits, a fairly difficult section because I always arrive too fast without realizing the speed I'm going. You get used to going so fast for such a long section that you leave your braking a bit late!

Jackie Ickx was born in Brussels on January 1st, 1945. He began his motoring career at the age of 16, first with scramble motorcycles, then with cars. Discovered by Ken Tyrrell, he was European Formula 2 champion in 1967 and in 1968 was taken on by Ferrari. He went over to Brabham in 1969, and went back to the Maranello team the following year, finally splitting from Ferrari halfway through the 1973 season and joining Lotus in 1974. He has many victories to his credit, both in Formula 1 and in world sports car championship races. A cool, calculating driver, he has a superb style.

Spa Francorchamps

Motor racing is a popular sport in Belgium, and one could say that almost all the roads in the country have been used at one time or another for racing. The Spa circuit was used for the first time in 1924, when a group of enthusiasts led by the president of the sports committee of the RACB, Henri Langlois van Ophem, decided to use the roads that between them linked the villages of Francorchamps, Malmédy and Stavelot in a charming valley in the Ardennes. The inaugural race was a 24-hour event for touring cars, and was won by Springel-Becquet in a Bignan at an average speed of 48·67 mph.

In the following year the first Belgian Grand Prix was run on the same circuit. As if to demonstrate the toughness of the course, only two cars crossed the finishing line on this occasion, the Alfa Romeos of Antonio Ascari and his team-mate Campari. The Spa-Francorchamps circuit continued to be the venue for motor and motorcycle races every year, but the Belgian Grand Prix was not contested on it again until 1930. With the passing of the years the circuit underwent various improvements, as has been the case with all the world's great circuits, subjected as they are to the critical eye of one organizer after another. On the whole, however, the circuit retained roughly the same characteristics, with the fast Eau Rouge, Malmédy and Stavelot bends, and the La Source switchback on the crest of a hill.

These were the glorious, heroic days of motor racing, when the greatest drivers of the time came to pit their wits against the tricky roads of the Belgian circuit. Some of them died here, among the forests of the Ardennes, notably Dick Seaman, who hit a tree head-on at the bend before La Source. The English driver's Mercedes caught fire and Seaman did not survive the injuries he received, dying shortly afterwards in hospital. People were already talking about the dangers of the circuit, though for the drivers it was like a magnet whose attraction they could not resist, for it was a fast and very testing course. Thus races were held on the track right up to the eve of the Second World War, which brought racing to a full stop at Spa-Francorchamps as it did at the majority of other European circuits.

When racing was re-started several modifications were made to the original circuit. Re-laying the surface enabled higher speeds to be attained and the remaking of some of the bends significantly reduced lap times.

The roll of drivers who lost their lives on what had become the Circuit

National de Francorchamps became frighteningly longer. In 1958 Archie Scott-Brown, a well-known Scottish driver, died in the blazing wreck of his car only just short of the spot where Seaman had lost his life eighteen years before. The similarity between the two accidents is almost uncanny, for in both cases the race was being run in the rain and in both cases the cars burst into flames on impact. The measures taken to improve the safety of the circuit were not in fact really adequate, as this aspect of motor racing was not at the time thought to be a major consideration. And the fact is that, in sad succession, Alan Stacey, Chris Bristow, Eric de Keyn, Wil Loos, Leon Dernier and Tony Hegbourne all died, while Stirling Moss and Jackie Stewart were both involved in accidents.

Times were changing, however, and the importance of safety was becoming a major issue among drivers, who had formed an association called the GPDA. One of the prime movers in the battle for increased safety measures on the world's circuits was Jackie Stewart, who in 1968 drew up a graduated list of circuits, pointing out shortcomings and the things that needed to be done to bring each circuit into line with the new safety requirements.

Stewart, outspoken as always, said: 'I believe that safety barriers are the only answer to Spa's problems and I think that these could be effectively employed without excessive expenditure on the part of the organization. They would not only make the circuit safer, but would also contribute to road safety, for these roads—which are open to daily traffic—would thus be made safer for the ordinary motorist. The thing that really creates problems at Spa is rain. It's not a matter of comparing our problems with those of the drivers of the past; perhaps on the straights they reached the same speeds as we do, but thanks to their tyres they were not in the least worried by the puddles, while we with our rain tyres can almost immediately tell when we are beginning to aquaplane. Driving over the roads with all those rivulets and puddles one gets the feeling that one has no control over the car whatsoever.'

Jack Brabham too, three times world champion and winner of the Belgian Grand Prix in 1960, expressed severe criticisms of the circuit in an article written in 1970: 'Spa is one of those unfortunate circuits that have become dangerous for racing in today's cars; in spite of this I very much enjoy driving on it because it presents such a rigorous test of a driver's skill. It is very, very fast and has a good surface, but with the latest developments in cars and tyres, and the sorts of speeds now reached, I think that Spa should cease to be used for Formula 1 races. It isn't really a matter of money either, as it is simply impossible to turn it into a safe track for the latest cars. As long as one stays on the road it's a marvellous circuit, but the risk of not staying on the road, at Spa, is very high. And when it's raining it's absurd to even think of driving on it.'

In 1971 Stewart, who in the meantime had become an influential member of the GPDA, pressed home the attack: 'In current terms the circuit is antiquated. There are a lot of defects in the bends, at Masta for example. You can be sure that even if some say they take it at full speed, nobody actually dares to do so. It's a dangerous circuit and we therefore treat it with respect. The main problem involved in making it safe lies in the fact that it passes through private property belonging to farmers who—justifiably— refuse to have their barbed wire cut because their livestock would escape. They also refuse to pay for the erection of safety barriers—and they're right.

Why should they? Even if guard rails were put up all the way round the circuit, the track would still be dangerous because of the high speeds we achieve on it. It only needs a puff of side wind to put one's car off course, and at that speed it's like a missile hurtling straight into the crowd. And that's something this sport can't afford.'

The controversy over Spa caused some ruptures in the Grand Prix Drivers' Association, and the Belgian driver Jacky Ickx left the association because of the dispute. Paul Frère, a Belgian former racing driver who had become a brilliant journalist, was one of Spa's most strenuous defenders. 'Because of its extremely fast course, made up for the most part of a series of bends that can be taken at 125 mph, Spa is the type of circuit that I consider ideal for Grand Prix racing. It's a course on which the fastest cars and the truly great drivers really stand out, and one which extracts the greatest performance from them. Because of its length and natural features the Circuit National de Francorchamps stands almost alone amidst the many mini-circuits that, for economic reasons to do with the astronomic cost of organizing a Grand Prix, have sprung up in recent years. Suspense is entirely lacking on these small circuits, while at Spa it is a natural ingredient. No other circuit in the world offers the public around the pits

area and the grandstands a view like the one offered from the end of La Source bend to the end of the slope up to Burnenville.'

The Spa circuit has therefore stood for some time at the centre of a dispute which without doubt even has political repercussions, for the drivers' ostracism of it has resulted in other circuits, recently opened in Belgium, receiving a greater share of the action. Notable among these is Nivelles, a mini-circuit which guarantees the maximum safety both to the spectators and to the competitors, but which, according to the experts is, all in all, a bit boring.

The GPDA campaign against the Ardennes circuit was pursued with ever-increasing vigour; so much so, in fact, that having forced the cancellation in 1969 and 1971 of the Belgian Grand Prix (failing Spa there were no other circuits adequate for the event), in 1972 and 1973 the drivers became even more directly involved when they were asked not to drive in the 1 000 Kilometres for Sports Cars either. Ferrari rather took the bull by the horns by deciding to go ahead and compete in the 1972 race, and in the event nearly all the long-distance race drivers took part, apparently with a good deal of satisfaction. Redman, in particular, who had already won three times at Spa, had this to say: 'A fast lap on this circuit gives me more satisfaction than anything else.'

Although the Formula 1 Grand Prix is now run elsewhere, Spa still hosts the 1 000-Kilometre Sports Car race and the 24-Hour Touring Car race. The 1973 edition of the latter served to emphasize the dangers of the circuit, for three drivers—Joisten, Dubos and Larini—were killed in it.

All the same, Spa's supporters are unwilling to accept final defeat, and arc studying ways of radically altering the circuit. Perhaps the changes will destroy some of the features that gave Spa world renown, but at least this valley in the Ardennes will not lose touch with the world of motor racing.

The Spa-Francorchamps circuit lies in the heart of the Ardennes. The weather here is highly unreliable and it is not unusual for a race to start in sunshine and meet rain further down the track. The surrounding countryside is mainly meadowland.

The town of Spa lies a very few miles from the circuit, which links Francorchamps, Burnenville and Stavelot. Being a famous health resort, Spa is always crowded, and on race days the population can be increased tenfold. Tents spring up all round the circuit.

There are numerous bars and restaurants around the circuit where one can eat, drink and follow the racing, while behind the pits young enthusiasts mingle.

When the sun shines a lot of the
work of preparation is carried
on outdoors.

For motor-racing enthusiasts pre-race activities have a powerful attraction, and barriers have to be erected to keep them out of the areas where mechanics are working on the cars. The Ferrari pit is always a popular destination, especially when—as here—local hero Jackie Ickx is present. The races are run partly on public roads, so there is an almost infinite range of vantage points.

One of the best vantage points is on the rise after Eau Rouge. Here one can see the cars coming down from the crest of La Source, passing the pits, and negotiating the Eau Rouge esses. No wise spectator at Spa comes without his rainwear. The legend painted on the track at the end of the esses bears witness to the tremendous following Jackie Ickx has in Belgium.

Clay Regazzoni

A lap at Spa

Spa lives up to its reputation, as one of the most engaging and dangerous circuits—every metre has its snares. It is a 'driver's circuit', and one has to know it very well indeed to do a good lap time without going off the road.

Real road circuits are generally not very safe because, being common roads open to everyday traffic, they have depressions and little bumps which are a hazard to racing cars with very firm suspension. A little bump is enough to make a racing car fly off line. To these normal dangers of all road circuits, Spa adds the very high-speed straights and curves.

On each lap at Spa, one learns something, and knowing this a driver has to be continuously—even increasingly—alert. The racing lines are well defined, but when one has to change from them for overtaking or any other reason, he can find himself in trouble on an 'unfavourable' zone of the track. From this point of view, I think that

Spa is better suited to a Formula 1 race than an endurance event for sports cars or saloons, because with single-seaters one at least competes with cars of roughly the same power and against highly qualified drivers.

Although I am aware of its dangers, my opinion of Spa is not so drastic as Stewart's; he convinced many drivers that they should not race on the circuit, where he was once involved in a spectacular accident which could have had serious consequences.

On the other hand, I thoroughly agree with my colleagues about racing at Spa in wet conditions—when it rains the circuit become undrivable. This happens more often than one might think, and furthermore while the road may be dry at the pits area, it can be raining hard at the other end of the circuit. This is a very real problem, because one can find oneself on dry tyres which are quite unsuited to

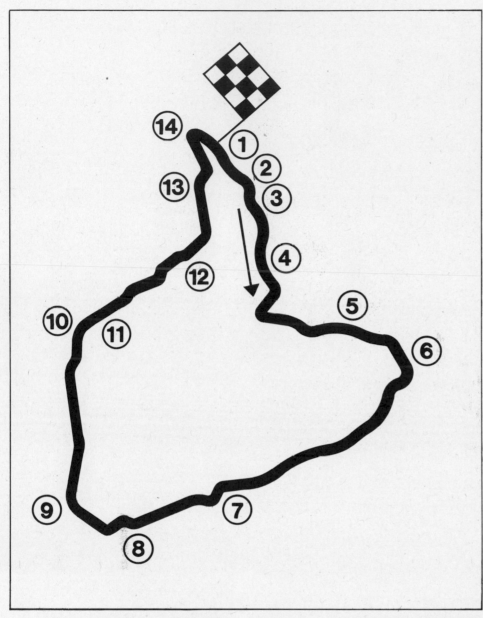

1 One takes the pits straight in fourth, forcing the pace. The track descends here, and the pits are protected by a low wall.

5 Heading for Burnenville, it is important to keep the car over on the outside, in 5th gear but not quite at full throttle.

9 Immediately after Holowell comes the new bend at Stavelot, the furthest point from the start.

10 Once round Stavelot, the drivers hit another very fast stretch, ending at the Carrières bend.

11 Now comes an almost straight stretch with white-walled houses beside it.

174

2 The downward slope ends at the bottom of the finishing straight, and the track rises again towards Eau Rouge, a particularly good vantage point.

3 The Eau Rouge grandstands, seen from the track. The right-hander rises to a very tortuous stretch leading to the Les Combes bend.

4 Immediately after the first Les Combes bend the track, rising gently, turns left and then drops down to the stretch immediately following.

6 This is the fastest stretch of the circuit, where the quickest cars reach 195–200 mph. It is called Burnenville.

7 This point is just before the Masta bend and here the drivers start to slow down, prior to taking the comparatively fast esses.

8 This is the approach to the Holowell bend, another esses taken fairly fast.

12 After some very fast bends, the drivers arrive at the Blanchimont bend, for which they throttle back a bit.

13 A short straight, two bends —a left-hander and a right-hander—then another short straight ending at La Source.

14 One has to brake hard for the La Source hairpin and takes it in 1st gear, then heads downhill for the finish.

slippery wet asphalt, with consequences that can be most unpleasant.

The most highly stressed part of a car racing at Spa is the engine, for it is required to run continuously at very high speeds. Vibrations can more often than not damage other components which are not strictly part of the transmission. Good road-holding qualities and aerodynamic shape are also very important, for it is a great advantage if a car is capable of achieving perhaps an additional 10 mph on the straights for any given power—this means that one is not bound to risk too much through the bends to put in a good lap time.

The pits at Spa are on a short descending straight, which on the flying lap is covered in fourth gear at maximum engine speed. At the bottom of the hill there is a bend turning left, then a right which is taken in third gear, in preparation for the climb which follows it. When the road levels out again, there are two very fast fourth gear 'ess' bends and then the Les Combes bend. This is a third gear corner, and after it one changes into fourth, then fifth, for the long straights in the slight descent towards Stavelot, one of the key bends on the circuit.

This long stretch calls for delicacy, in part because the road undulates; the most difficult parts ore the bends at Burnenville and Malmédy, negotiated at well over 150 mph, and the Masta, which is a kink rather than a corner. Here there are cottages on both sides and it is not amusing to speed between the rigid safety barriers at over 180 mph! An instant of hesitation, or a slower car to be lapped, can cost dear, while if one releases the throttle pedal too soon or too much one can lose too many engine revolutions. The whole stretch demands complete attention, and there is also the unnerving distraction of a valley on the right.

Stavelot comprises two bends to the right, connected by another short slope. The first is downhill, and the road camber is adverse. There are several traps. Enter the first bend too fast and you can either leave the track, or be badly placed for the second; if one goes in too slowly the whole lap time can be compromised, because after Stavelot there are straights which call for very high speeds, and the faster one comes out of the corner, the better.

From Stavelot up through la Carrière to la Source one travels at about 180 mph, along straights linked by high-speed bends, some of them very fast ess bends. Before the sharp la Source right-hander leading back to the pits straight one has to brake very strongly, for it is impossible to take this at more than about 45 mph. One cannot go faster as this corner is on a road

junction, and the two roads join at different inclinations.

That completes the lap, and one descends past the pits again without having a moment for the attention to wander. Rest is possible only when one stops at the pits to hand over the car to a team mate.

Clay Regazzoni, born at Lugano on September 5th, 1939, owes his fame to his seasons with the Ferrari team. To a meteoric performance in Formula 2 (he was European champion in 1970 with a Tecno) he added major successes in Formula 1, including winning the Italian GP at Monza. In 1973 he joined BRM when the Ferrari team was cut back, but he returned to the Italian team in 1974. He is a fast, dashing and courageous driver.

Watkins Glen

The idea of building a circuit at Watkins Glen came to Cameron
Argetsinger at the end of 1947 when, with his wife and sons, he visited
Watkins Glen and the adjoining State Park. For a long time, Argetsinger
had been nursing the idea of bringing road racing back to the United
States, and even before he had met anybody who could help him to realize
his dream, he mapped out a circuit at Watkins Glen. It was to be a proper
road circuit, with all kinds of bends, gradients and surfaces. On a scrap of
paper he pencilled in a line that went from the main street of Watkins Glen
towards Corning Hill and crossed Watkins Glen State Park before turning
back towards the main street via a series of bends that led to Franklin
Street.

He took his rough plan to the officials of the authority administering the
little tourist centre near Lake Seneca. They liked the idea, for Argetsinger
stressed in the most convincing way the advantages in terms of tourism that
it would bring, and the possibility of prolonging the tourist season, which
he emphasized, tipped the scales in his favour; local businessmen and
hoteliers all came out on his side.

On October 2nd, 1948, the first postwar road race in America was run
on the 6·6-mile circuit, which snaked through the village of Glen. There
were fifteen competitors, and victory went to Frank Griswold in an Alfa
Romeo 2900 coupé. The event was a complete success, thanks to the efforts
of, among others, Alec Ulmann, a man whose name was soon to be linked
with the Sebring 12 Hours. Many of the competitors in the first race at the
Glen were wealthy amateurs, who spent their time racing much as others
did playing polo or deep-sea fishing. Only one accident, and that fortunately
without injury, took place: Bill Milliken, who later became a member of the
Glen's board of directors, hurtled off the road at a corner which was
immediately christened 'Milliken's corner'. Another competitor in this first
contest was Cameron Argetsinger, whose MG TC finished in ninth place.

In the following year the race attracted 58 entrants and more than
20 000 spectators, four times the number that had attended the inaugural
race. To cater for the greater number of competitors, heats were organized
for the various categories of cars entered. Argetsinger and his associates had
a lot to be pleased about.

The third meeting at the Glen, on the other hand, was a black day for the organizers. Sam Collier, at the wheel of a Ferrari, ran off the road just as he was going into a bend flanked by a field. The car turned over and over, and the efforts of those who rescued the driver and rushed him to hospital were in vain. There were two more accidents during the meeting, both fortunately less serious, and at the end of the proceedings outgoings were found to have exceeded receipts by $1 000. All this made the organizers wonder whether they should abandon the enterprise altogether.

As if to add yet one more difficulty, censures were received from the Sport Car Club of America and the American Automobile Association, following the fatal accident. As a protest against the attitude of these two bodies Argetsinger resigned from the board and his place was taken by Lester Smalley, one of the principal champions of road racing.

Things went forward: in 1951 no accidents were recorded in the races, but in the following year something happened that was to spell the end of the road circuit. With the ever-growing number of spectators it became almost impossible to control the crowd—and the inevitable happened.

On the second lap of the main race, Fred Wacker's car skidded in the Corning Hill area, hit a kerb, made a brief excursion off the road and then got back into the race. What the driver did not realize was that he had knocked down thirteen people! A seven-year-old child was killed, and the other twelve sustained injuries. The race was stopped immediately, but inevitably this accident aroused vehement criticism against motor racing from every quarter: 'It is time to put an end to the orgy of violence and blood,' one newspaper exhorted, while others echoed this sentiment, asserting that the spectators travelled hundreds of miles with the sole purpose of seeing accidents and blood.

The Watkins Glen organizers decided to sit it out until things quietened down, which, after a few weeks, they did. But the worst blow had still to fall: without warning Lloyds of London, who had provided insurance cover for the first races, withdrew it, stating that they would only reconsider their position if a way could be found of stopping the spectators getting too close to the track. This spelt the end of the first Watkins Glen circuit.

Yet the board of directors had no intention of abandoning their sporting enterprise. They found a rectangle of roads a few miles distant from the village, and raised the $25 000 needed to provide the necessary auxiliaries and a new surface for the roads.

From 1953 to 1955 the October race meeting was held on this 'transitional' circuit, but it was soon realized that the circuit could not meet the needs of either the competitors or the spectators, the latter because it did not offer them adequate service or facilities. It was at this time that Milliken, who had always given the organizers his advice and collaboration, suggested that they should build a permanent circuit. His proposal was received with great interest and the Grand Prix Corporation decided to acquire a large piece of land in the vicinity of Watkins Glen. As could easily have been foreseen, the task of planning the circuit was entrusted to Milliken, who boasted a successful racing career and therefore could be relied upon to create an interesting course. Also called in to collaborate in this task was a group belonging to the Engineering Department of Cornell University.

The circuit, 2·3 miles long, was laid out in the hilly area chosen by the organizers and was completed at a cost of some $200 000. Work on it finished the day before practice for the 1956 meeting was due to start, and this posed an unexpected problem: the track surface had not set fully and crumbled as the tyres did their work. Tiny pebbles were therefore thrown up, smashing a number of windscreens and the headlights of practically all the cars using the track.

The Sports Car Club of America immediately forebade the competitors to race and thus take unnecessary risks; the drivers, however, chose to take matters into their own hands and the race was run without incident.

Meanwhile interest in 'European-style' racing was increasing rapidly in America, and some American drivers had earned places as members of English or Italian works teams. Eventually, the United States Grand Prix became a world championship event, run at Sebring in 1959 and in 1960. As it was the only circuit within a five hour drive of New York, Watkins Glen was a natural venue for this event, and since 1961 the United States Grand Prix has become a regular fixture there.

After the Grand Prix, the organizers began to get interested in the international sports car championship as well, and they launched a six-hour race which they wanted to have inserted in the international racing calendar; this was achieved, even though there were already two sports car championship fixtures in America, at Daytona and Sebring. It was thus that in 1968 a second world championship race took its place in Watkins Glen's annual calendar. One year later a Canada-America Trophy race, better known as the Can-Am championship, also found its way into the

programme. Only ten years after its debut in the world of motor sport, Watkins Glen had joined the big league.

Further modifications were made to the circuit, particularly with a view to making things more comfortable for the ever-growing numbers of race fans who flocked to the meetings. Among the changes made in the interests of the competitors, the most impressive is the Kendall Service Center, a larger building housing the cars of the various teams and providing excellent working conditions for the mechanics. For safety's sake several thousand yards of guard rails were erected, while further grandstands were built and a number of subways installed.

In spite of all this, the drivers were not entirely happy. In 1968 Jackie Stewart was asked by the Grand Prix Drivers' Association to examine and comment on the world's principal circuits. Of Watkins Glen he said: 'At this circuit the most serious problem is that of the safety of the spectators. There are a lot of police around the start area, but generally not enough elsewhere. What once happened to me was that I had to brake, while racing, to avoid a pair of spectators who were crossing the track! Then there is the question of the pits, which I don't think have been very well planned, especially when one considers how lap speeds are progressively escalating. In fact on practice days one often reaches the top of the rise after the finishing line to find oneself confronted by another competitor who, having just left the pits, is moving at a much slower speed. The best thing to do would be to transfer the pits to the straight, a much safer location for them.'

It was at the end of 1970 that a decision was taken, perhaps influenced to some degree by the drivers' criticisms, to rebuild the track, including lengthening it by a good mile. This cost about 3·5 million dollars altogether and, with the modernization of the entire establishment, was sufficient to satisfy all parties.

The track was completely redesigned, the pits were resited along the grandstand straight, camping areas with all necessary facilities were organized, and yet more grandstands and subways were built. Additionally, safety nets were erected for the protection of spectators.

Nor was the track surface neglected, this being widened and resurfaced. The layout of the circuit was subjected to the examination of a computer at Cornell University. Once the average lap speed desired had been established, all relevant data on the current Formula One cars were fed to the computer, together with the other information needed for it to offer a full answer on the features of the track. Thus with the help of the computer the radius of all the bends and the length of every straight were determined. According to the electronic brain the cars would reach a speed of 178 mph at the end of the longest straights.

On the first day's practice on the new circuit Stewart in his Tyrrell-Ford clocked up this same 178 mph on the photoelectric cell at the end of the longest straight—so the computer was dead right—but it had been fed one wrong piece of information: the desired average speed had been 100 mph, but in 1971 Francois Cevert won at an average of 114·26 mph.

Apart from this duel at a distance between the computer and the drivers' skills, the new Watkins Glen circuit has emerged victorious from every test and thus may be added to the distinguished roll of those circuits that have been able to keep up with the galloping development of motor racing technology and the changing requirements of drivers and spectators.

U.S. GRAND PRIX
WATKINS GLEN
OCTOBER 8, 1972

Watkins Glen scenes.
Opposite page, top left;
portable toilets. Top right; the
Goodyear bus, equipped as a
rest room for drivers. Middle
right; single-seater transporters.
Bottom; a horseback police
patrol.

Left and above left; two views of the garages, much frequented by enthusiasts. Above; souvenir selling again. Above right; a caricature of Graham Hill on his Brabham's wing. Below; Stewart's Tyrrell-Ford undergoing a thorough checkover before practice, in the capacious garage. Opposite page, top; the youth band practises prior to the presentation of the teams. Centre left; the big glass building that houses all the services. Centre right; spectators strolling on the track before the race, in front of the beflagged grandstand. Bottom left; drums of Texaco fuel for the individual teams. It is interesting to note that it is also used by the Tyrrell team, which, being sponsored by the French Elf petrol company, might be expected to use the latter's products. Bottom right; practice in full swing. Here Regazzoni's Ferrari leads Graham Hill's Brabham.

Opposite, top; local idol Peter Revson in the McLaren pits during practice, with one of his aerofoils being adjusted. Centre, the abbreviated names of the drivers lying ready to be used for in-race signals. Far left; before the race some people wander about while others prefer to relax on the ground. Left; a view of the grandstand area. This page, top; the race is on. A spectator wearing ear-protectors. Above; François Cevert, number two in the Tyrrell-Ford team, in action. Right; a tree solves some visibility problems.

Cars tightly grouped in the initial stages of the race. Note how big the run-off areas are. There are no guard rails, protective netting at the edge of these wide grass strips being used instead. On the left, Jackie Stewart kisses his wife after winning the United States Grand Prix.

Ronnie Peterson

A lap at Watkins Glen

Watkins Glen is a circuit I enjoy very much, in fact it's in my top seven along with the Nürburgring, Interlagos, Clermont-Ferrand, Barcelona, Monaco and Mosport. I usually seem to go pretty well at the Glen, and I think it's got some fairly interesting and difficult corners which make it quite satisfying. The safety precautions are very good, as are the pits, and the surface is very smooth, apart from two rough sections.

On a flying lap I come out of the corner before the pits in third gear and select fourth just before the start/finish line. The first corner, the '90', is just that, and is approached from the far left of the track. I brake and go straight into second gear and take a fairly late apex before applying full power in second and drifting right out to the kerb at the border of the track. I then select third almost immediately, and then, without taking the engine up to full revs, change into fourth, so that I need

not make any gear changes through the next three corners. The three corners comprising 'Graham Hill' are probably the most important on the circuit, and if this section is taken well, a fast run down the back straight is ensured and you're half the way towards making a fast lap time. I try to point the car through the corners as much as possible, keeping close to the inside so as to avoid sliding on the gravel and oil which always seem to accumulate on the outside. It is very easy to clip the kerb on the left hand part of Graham Hill, but this should be avoided because it upsets the car too much; through slower corners this doesn't really matter, but when accelerating hard in fourth gear it's very easy to spin. I did this once, but I was using a set of unscrubbed tyres at the time. However, Graham Hill is a very enjoyable section of the track, and being bordered by very high triple-layer armco, it has a similar feeling to driving round the

1 The pits straight is not very long and is taken in 4th gear. At the far end of it is a bend called '90' because it turns through 90 degrees.

2 This short straight is followed by a very elongated esses, the most testing part of the circuit. Here the drivers select 4th gear.

3 Leaving the last of the three bends in the esses puts one on a long descending straight which is taken in 5th gear.

7 The U-bend which leads on to a short straight before the final series of bends. Precious fractions of seconds can be gained here.

8 Going downhill, one comes to a right-hander that seems much sharper than it is. At this point single seaters are in 4th gear.

9 This is the fast bend leading on to the grandstand straight. Drivers generally take it in 3rd, turning at the last possible moment.

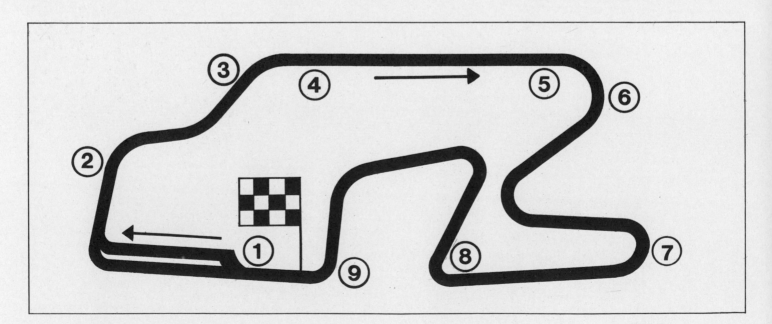

4
The surface at the beginning of the straight opposite the finishing straight is very rough and makes the car vibrate. Here one is travelling at top speed.

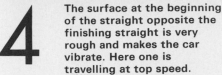

5
This downhill stretch leads to the tricky bend called the Loop, difficult because it exits downwards. There are guard rails on both sides.

6
After negotiating the Loop the drivers come to another bend. There is a little 'hop' where the new track intersects the old.

The Swedish Ronnie Peterson, born at Orebro on February 14th, 1944, has had a meteoric career, graduating from Karts to Formula 1 in the space of three years (1967–1970). Considered the most promising driver of the new generation, he became European Formula 2 champion in 1971. A courageous driver, Ronnie was asked by Colin Chapman at the beginning of 1973 to join the Lotus team, together with Emerson Fittipaldi. He won his first Grand Prix in France.

191

'armco funnel' at Barcelona. I change into fifth gear just before the end of the corner and then the car passes over a very rough section of track and everything vibrates.

Down the straight in fifth gear, towards the Loop, which is a fairly difficult corner with a downhill exit. Most of the overtaking is done at the end of the straight, and I usually brake just after a hump and with the car positioned in the centre of the track. I usually brake by instinct and very rarely use marker boards. I turn into the Loop fairly early, keeping the car close to the inside and then drift out downhill in fourth gear. Just after you come out of the corner the road crosses part of the old track and there is quite a bump, but then you continue downhill in fourth and then brake hard for the left-hander which is taken in third. Because you are running downhill it is important to be delicate with the brakes so that the tail doesn't jump out of line. Out of the left-hander I slide right to the edge of the track, where again there always seems to be a lot of oil and dust, and then change into fourth before braking and selecting second gear for the tight right-hander. This corner is quite unusual because the road is uphill as you come out so I get the power on early and use all the road. This is another section where it is possible to make up time, because if you are following someone closely and come out of this corner quicker it is possible to pass under braking at the end of the next straight.

Out of the right-hander I change into third gear and then select fourth before braking downhill (again) for a right-hander which seems tighter than it really is—probably because we approach it downhill. I take second for this corner, keeping well to the inside with an early apex and making sure that I don't slide too much before the left-hander which follows. I accelerate into third out of the right-hander, then change down to second for the left-hander and then quickly back into third again. The left-hander is always very slippery so it's important to keep to the inside as much as possible. I stay in third gear down the short straight which follows and then into the next left-hander I take an early apex earlier, I think, than most drivers. I slide to the outside of this corner and then move straight over to the other side of the road for the next right-hander, for which I also take a late apex; I then accelerate out past the pits in third and fourth gears.

The major races

The major races

Lotus

1972

E. Fittipaldi
112.06 mph

Brands Hatch

British Grand Prix

1964

Lotus

Clark
94.14 mph

Brabham

1966

Brabham
95.48 mph

1968

Lotus

Siffert
104.83 mph

1970

Lotus

Rindt
108.69 mph

Brands Hatch

Sports cars

1967

Chaparral

P. Hill-Spence
93.08 mph

Ford

1968

Ickx-Redman
95.96 mph

Porsche

1969

Siffert-Redman
100.22 mph

1970   **Porsche**

Rodriguez-Kinnunen
92.15 mph

Alfa Romeo

1971

de Adamich -
Pescarolo
97.17 mph

1972   **Ferrari**

Ickx-Andretti
105.12 mph

Buenos Aires

Argentine Grand Prix

1953   **Ferrari**

Alberto Ascari
78.14 mph

Maserati   **1954**

Fangio
70.13 mph

1955   **Mercedes**

Fangio
77.51 mph

Ferrari   **1956**

Fangio-Musso
79.38 mph

1957   **Maserati**

Fangio
80.47 mph

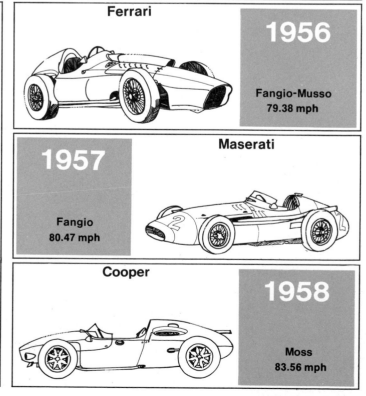

Cooper   **1958**

Moss
83.56 mph

213

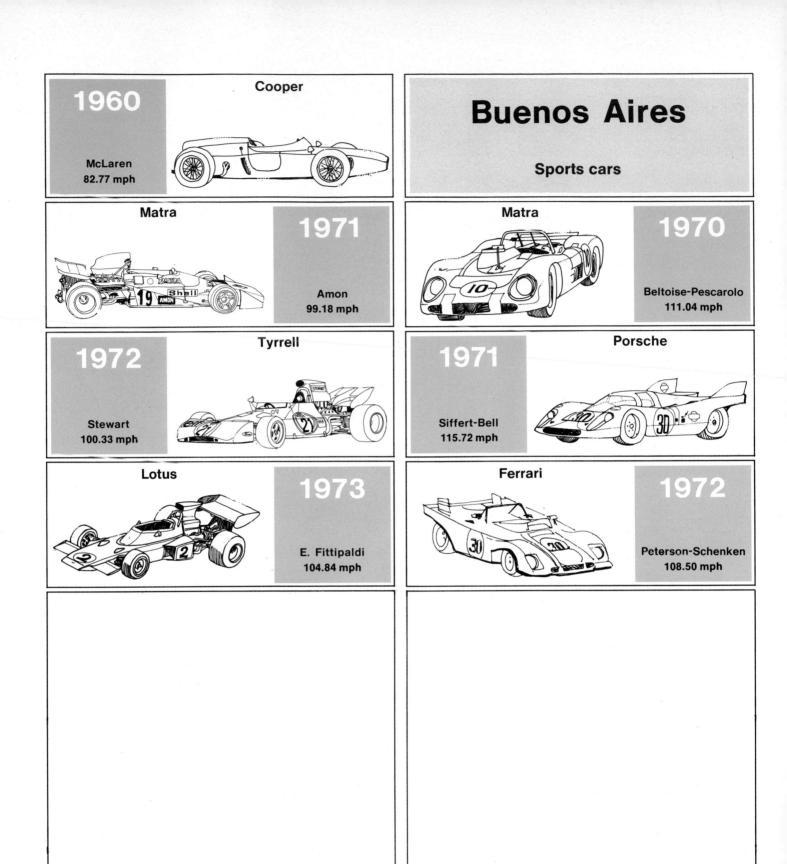

1960 Cooper
McLaren
82.77 mph

Buenos Aires

Sports cars

Matra **1971**
Amon
99.18 mph

Matra **1970**
Beltoise-Pescarolo
111.04 mph

1972 Tyrrell
Stewart
100.33 mph

1971 Porsche
Siffert-Bell
115.72 mph

Lotus **1973**
E. Fittipaldi
104.84 mph

Ferrari **1972**
Peterson-Schenken
108.50 mph

Indianapolis

Indianapolis 500 miles

1919 Peugeot
Wilcox
88.05 mph

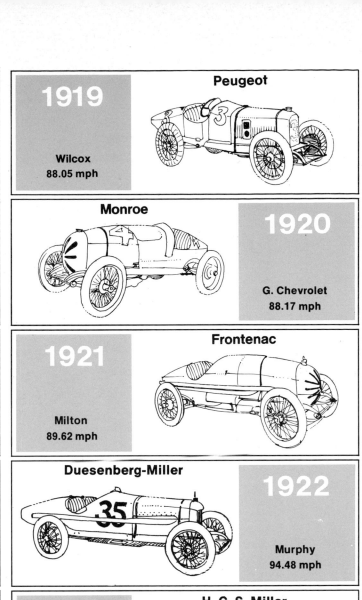

Marmon "Wasp"
1911
Harroun-Patschke
74.59 mph

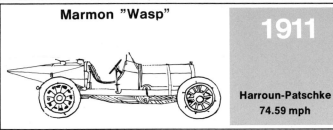

Monroe **1920**
G. Chevrolet
88.17 mph

1912 National
Dawson-Herr
78.72 mph

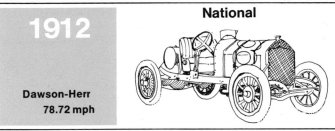

1921 Frontenac
Milton
89.62 mph

Peugeot **1913**
Goux
75.93 mph

Duesenberg-Miller **1922**
Murphy
94.48 mph

1914 Delage
Thomas
82.47 mph

1923 H. C. S. Miller
Milton-Wilcox
90.95 mph

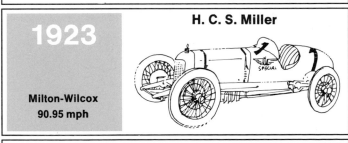

Mercedes **1915**
De Palma
89.84 mph

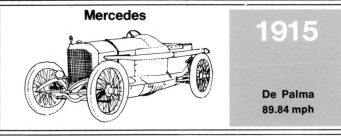

Duesenberg **1924**
Corum-Boyer
98.23 mph

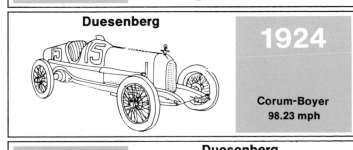

1916 Peugeot
Resta
84.00 mph

1925 Duesenberg
De Paolo-Batten
101.13 mph

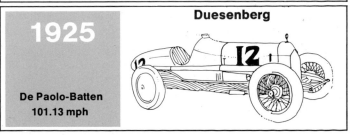

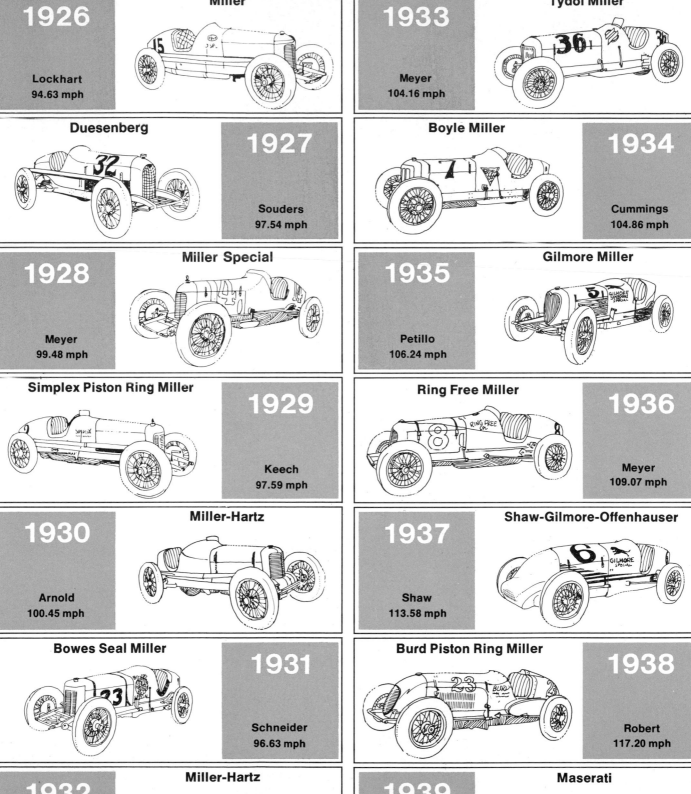

1926 Lockhart 94.63 mph — Miller	**1933** Meyer 104.16 mph — Tydol Miller
Duesenberg — **1927** Souders 97.54 mph	Boyle Miller — **1934** Cummings 104.86 mph
1928 Meyer 99.48 mph — Miller Special	**1935** Petillo 106.24 mph — Gilmore Miller
Simplex Piston Ring Miller — **1929** Keech 97.59 mph	Ring Free Miller — **1936** Meyer 109.07 mph
1930 Arnold 100.45 mph — Miller-Hartz	**1937** Shaw 113.58 mph — Shaw-Gilmore-Offenhauser
Bowes Seal Miller — **1931** Schneider 96.63 mph	Burd Piston Ring Miller — **1938** Robert 117.20 mph
1932 Frame 104.14 mph — Miller-Hartz	**1939** Shaw 115.04 mph — Maserati

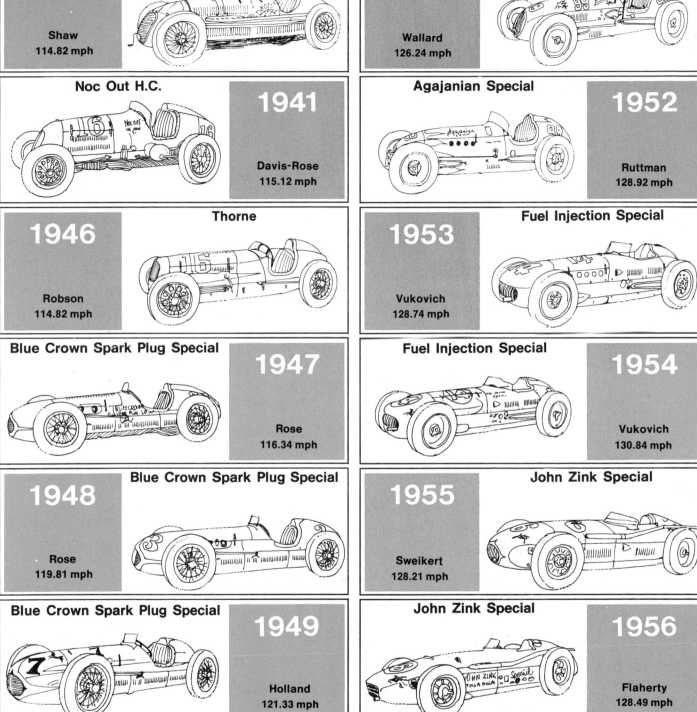

1940 Maserati
Shaw
114.82 mph

1951 Belanger Special
Wallard
126.24 mph

Noc Out H.C. **1941**
Davis-Rose
115.12 mph

Agajanian Special **1952**
Ruttman
128.92 mph

1946 Thorne
Robson
114.82 mph

1953 Fuel Injection Special
Vukovich
128.74 mph

Blue Crown Spark Plug Special **1947**
Rose
116.34 mph

Fuel Injection Special **1954**
Vukovich
130.84 mph

1948 Blue Crown Spark Plug Special
Rose
119.81 mph

1955 John Zink Special
Sweikert
128.21 mph

Blue Crown Spark Plug Special **1949**
Holland
121.33 mph

John Zink Special **1956**
Flaherty
128.49 mph

1950 Wynn's Friction Proofing Special
Parsons
124.00 mph

1957 Belond Exhaust Special
Hanks
135.60 mph

217

1958   **Belond AP Special 1**

Bryan
133.79 mph

Leader Card 500 Roadster   **1959**

Ward
135.86 mph

1960   **Ken Paul Special**

Rathmann
138.77 mph

Bowes Seal Fast Special   **1961**

Foyt
139.13 mph

1962   **Leader Card 500 Roadster**

Ward
140.29 mph

Agajanian Willard Special   **1963**

Parnelli Jones
143.14 mph

1964   **Sheraton Thompson Special**

Foyt
147.26 mph

1965   **Lotus-Ford**

Clark
150.68 mph

American Red Ball Special Lola   **1966**

G. Hill
144.32 mph

1967   **Sheraton-Thompson Special**

Foyt
151.21 mph

Rislone Special   **1968**

B. Unser
152.88 mph

1969   **STP Oil Treatment Special**

Andretti
156.87 mph

Johnny Lightning 500 Special   **1970**

A. Unser
155.75 mph

1971   **Johnny Lightning 500 Special**

A. Unser
157.74 mph

1972

Sunoco-McLaren

Donohue
162.96 mph

Eagle-STP

1973

Johncock
159.02 mph

Kyalami

South African Grand Prix

Cooper

1967

P. Rodriguez
97.10 mph

1968

Lotus

Clark
107.42 mph

Matra

1969

Stewart
110.62 mph

1970

Brabham

Brabham
111.70 mph

Ferrari

1971

Andretti
112.36 mph

McLaren

1972

Hulme
114.23 mph

Tyrrell

1973

Stewart
117.20 mph

La Lorraine

1925

de Courcelles-
Rossignol
57.83 mph

1926

La Lorraine

Bloch-Rossignol
66.08 mph

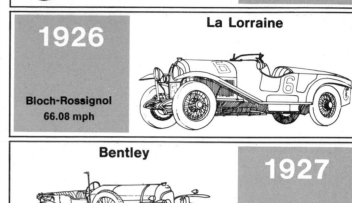

Bentley

1927

Benjafield-Davis
61.35 mph

1928

Bentley

Barnato-Rubin
69.11 mph

Bentley

1929

Barnato-Birkin
73.63 mph

Le Mans

Le Mans 24-hour Race

1923

Chenard-Walcker

Legache-Léonard
57.20 mph

1930

Bentley

Barnato-Kidston
75.88 mph

Bentley

1924

Duff-Clement
58.78 mph

Alfa Romeo

1931

Howe-Birkin
78.13 mph

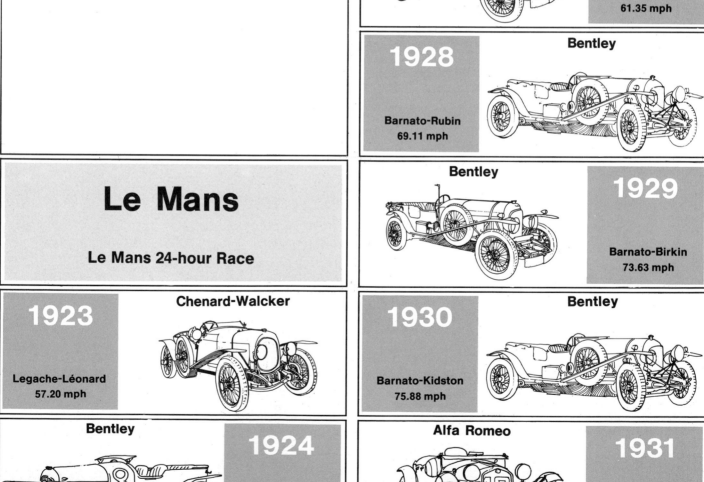

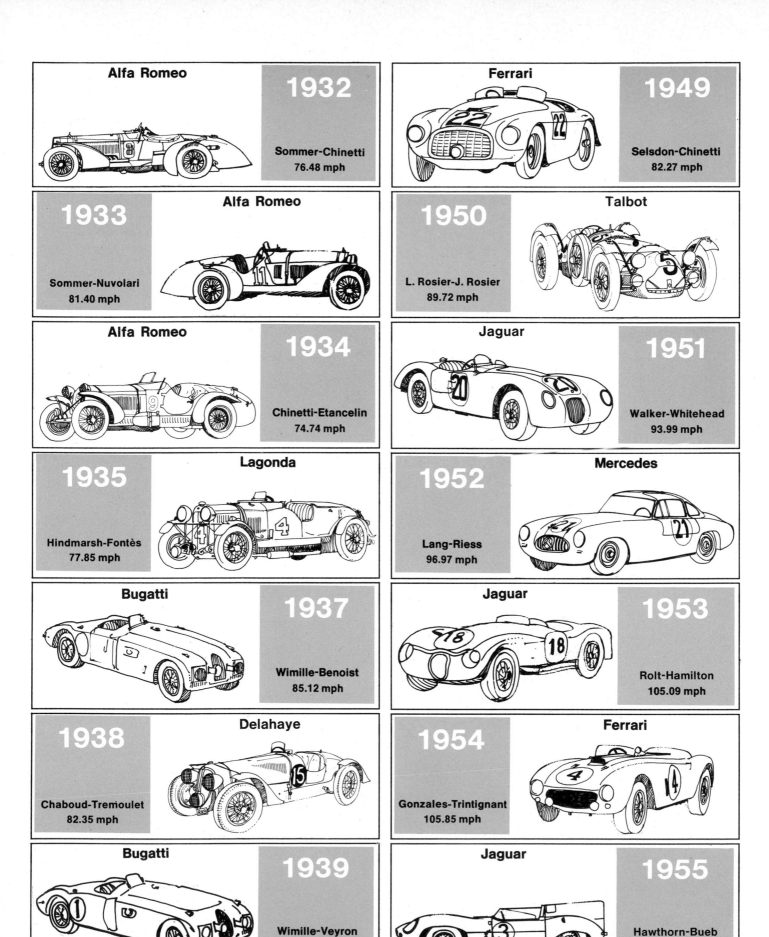

Alfa Romeo
1932
Sommer-Chinetti
76.48 mph

Ferrari
1949
Selsdon-Chinetti
82.27 mph

1933
Alfa Romeo
Sommer-Nuvolari
81.40 mph

1950
Talbot
L. Rosier-J. Rosier
89.72 mph

Alfa Romeo
1934
Chinetti-Etancelin
74.74 mph

Jaguar
1951
Walker-Whitehead
93.99 mph

1935
Lagonda
Hindmarsh-Fontès
77.85 mph

1952
Mercedes
Lang-Riess
96.97 mph

Bugatti
1937
Wimille-Benoist
85.12 mph

Jaguar
1953
Rolt-Hamilton
105.09 mph

1938
Delahaye
Chaboud-Tremoulet
82.35 mph

1954
Ferrari
Gonzales-Trintignant
105.85 mph

Bugatti
1939
Wimille-Veyron
86.85 mph

Jaguar
1955
Hawthorn-Bueb
106.99 mph

Jaguar	**1956**	**Ferrari**	**1963**
	Flockhart-Sanderson 104.46 mph		Scarfiotti-Bandini 118.10 mph

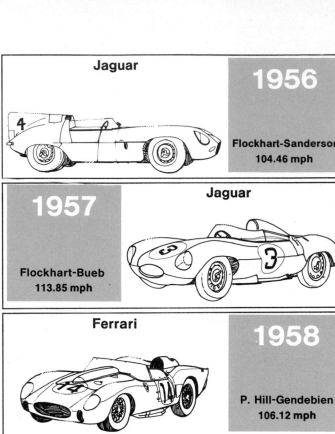

1957 **Jaguar**

Flockhart-Bueb
113.85 mph

1964 **Ferrari**

Guichet-Vaccarella
121.60 mph

Ferrari **1958**

P. Hill-Gendebien
106.12 mph

Ferrari **1965**

Gregory-Rindt
121.80 mph

1959 **Aston Martin**

Salvadori-Shelby
112.57 mph

1966 **Ford**

Amon-McLaren
125.41 mph

Ferrari **1960**

Frère-Gendebien
109.20 mph

Ford **1967**

Gurney-Foyt
135.78 mph

1961 **Ferrari**

Gendebien-P. Hill
115.93 mph

1968 **Ford**

P. Rodriguez-
L. Bianchi
117.93 mph

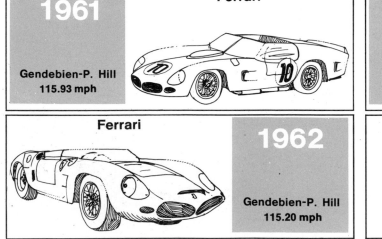

Ferrari **1962**

Gendebien-P. Hill
115.20 mph

Ford **1969**

Ickx-Oliver
129.40 mph

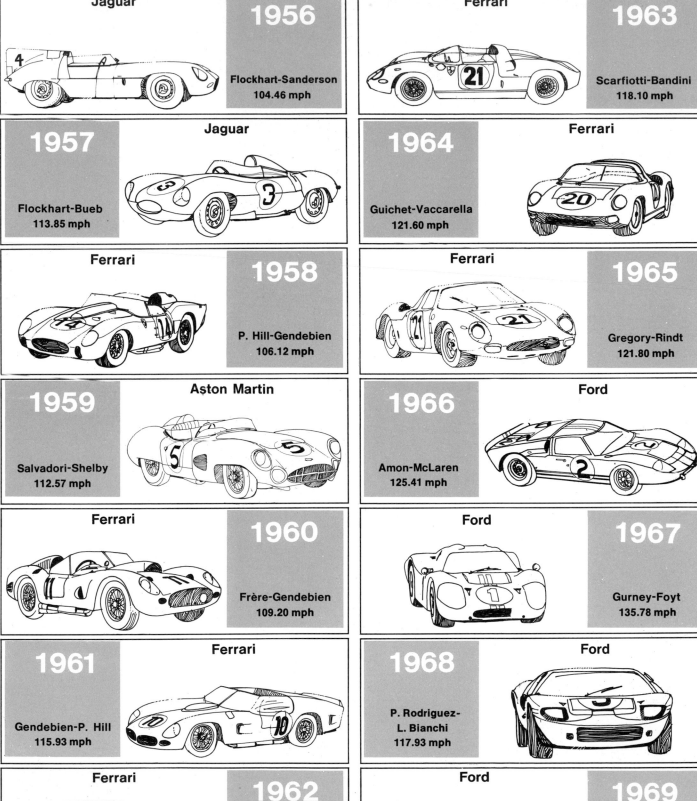

Porsche

1970

Attwood-Herrmann
119.29 mph

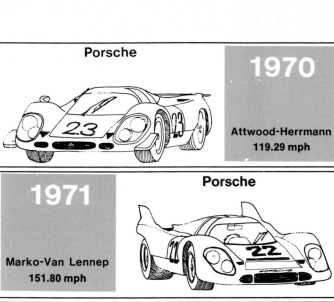

1971

Porsche

Marko-Van Lennep
151.80 mph

Matra

1972

Pescarolo-G. Hill
121.46 mph

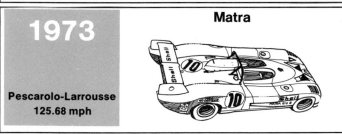

1973

Matra

Pescarolo-Larrousse
125.68 mph

Montecarlo

Monaco Grand Prix

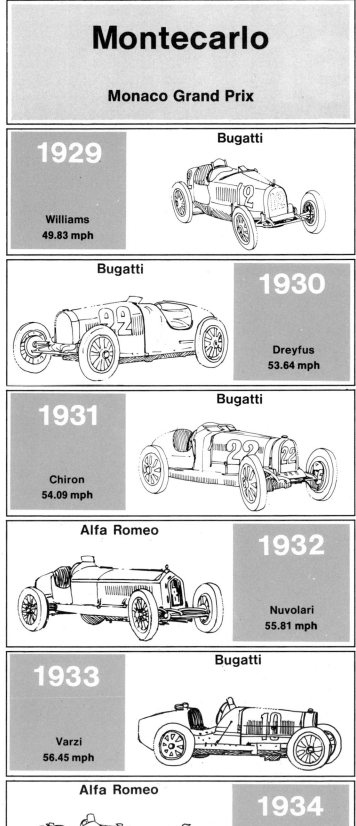

Bugatti

1929

Williams
49.83 mph

Bugatti

1930

Dreyfus
53.64 mph

Bugatti

1931

Chiron
54.09 mph

Alfa Romeo

1932

Nuvolari
55.81 mph

1933

Bugatti

Varzi
56.45 mph

Alfa Romeo

1934

Moll
56.05 mph

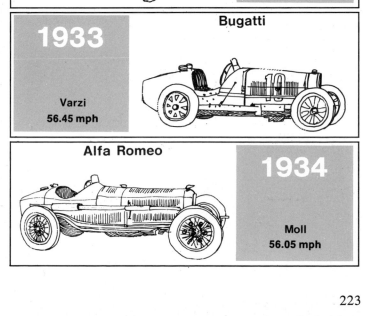

223

1935   Mercedes

Fagioli
55.17 mph

1956   Maserati

Moss
64.95 mph

Mercedes   **1936**

Caracciola
51.69 mph

Maserati   **1957**

Fangio
64.75 mph

1937   Mercedes

Von Brauchitsch
63.27 mph

1958   Cooper

Trintignant
67.98 mph

Maserati   **1948**

Farina
59.74 mph

Cooper   **1959**

Brabham
66.74 mph

1950   Alfa Romeo

Fangio
61.33 mph

1960   Lotus

Moss
67.46 mph

Ferrari (sports)   **1952**

Marzotto
58.20 mph

Lotus   **1961**

Moss
70.70 mph

1955   Ferrari

Trintignant
65.63 mph

Cooper   **1962**

McLaren
70.46 mph

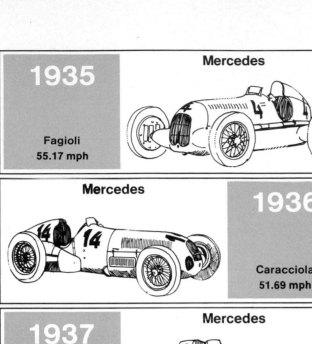
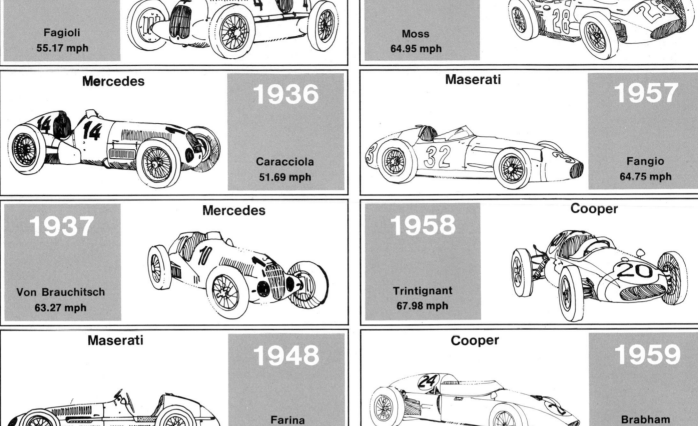

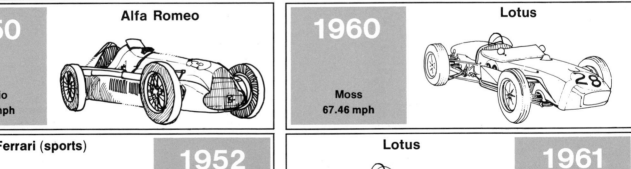
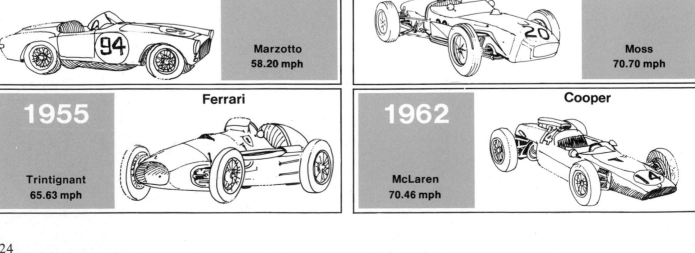

1963   BRM
G. Hill
72.42 mph

1964   BRM
G. Hill
72.64 mph

1965   BRM
G. Hill
74.30 mph

1966   BRM
Stewart
76.50 mph

1967   Brabham
Hulme
75.89 mph

1968   Lotus
G. Hill
77.82 mph

1969   Lotus
G. Hill
80.18 mph

1970   Lotus
Rindt
81.84 mph

1971   Tyrrell
Stewart
83.49 mph

1972   BRM
Beltoise
63.85 mph

1973   Tyrrell
Stewart
80.96 mph

Monza

Italian Grand Prix

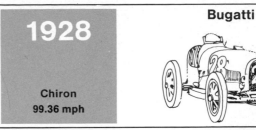

1928 Bugatti

Chiron
99.36 mph

Fiat **1922**

Bordino
86.90 mph

Maserati **1930**

Varzi
93.48 mph

1923 Fiat

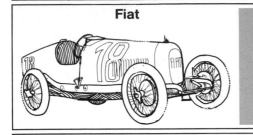

Salamano
91.03 mph

1931 Alfa Romeo

Nuvolari-Campari
96.79 mph

Alfa Romeo **1924**

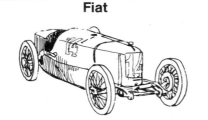

Antonio Ascari
98.79 mph

Alfa Romeo **1932**

Nuvolari
104.09 mph

1925 Alfa Romeo

Brilli-Peri
94.82 mph

1933 Alfa Romeo

Fagioli
108.58 mph

Bugatti **1926**

Charavel
85.88 mph

Mercedes **1934**

Fagioli-Caracciola
65.35 mph

1927 Delage

Benoist
90.05 mph

1935 Auto Union

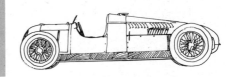

Stuck
85.18 mph

226

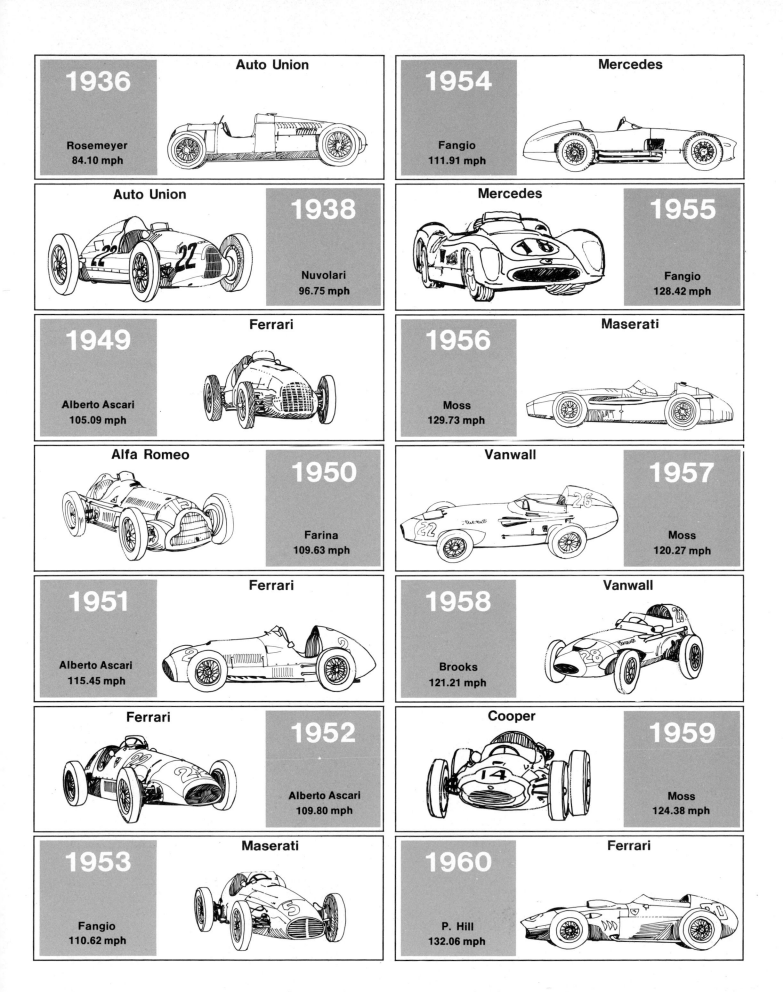

1936 Auto Union
Rosemeyer
84.10 mph

1938 Auto Union
Nuvolari
96.75 mph

1949 Ferrari
Alberto Ascari
105.09 mph

1950 Alfa Romeo
Farina
109.63 mph

1951 Ferrari
Alberto Ascari
115.45 mph

1952 Ferrari
Alberto Ascari
109.80 mph

1953 Maserati
Fangio
110.62 mph

1954 Mercedes
Fangio
111.91 mph

1955 Mercedes
Fangio
128.42 mph

1956 Maserati
Moss
129.73 mph

1957 Vanwall
Moss
120.27 mph

1958 Vanwall
Brooks
121.21 mph

1959 Cooper
Moss
124.38 mph

1960 Ferrari
P. Hill
132.06 mph

227

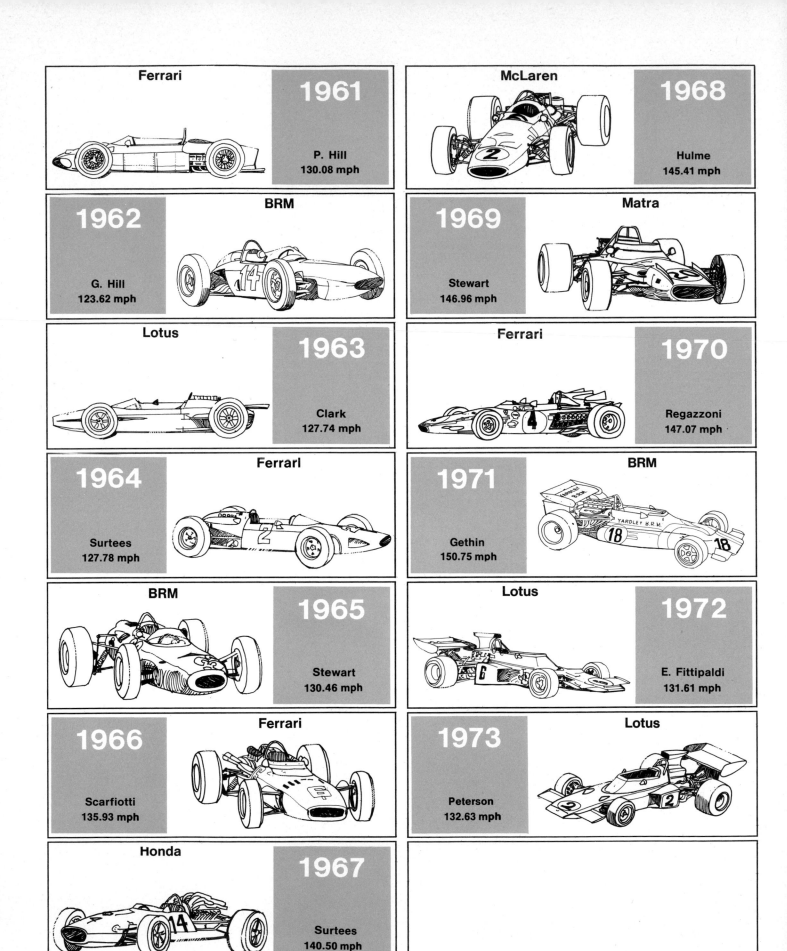

Ferrari — **1961** — P. Hill 130.08 mph

McLaren — **1968** — Hulme 145.41 mph

1962 — **BRM** — G. Hill 123.62 mph

1969 — **Matra** — Stewart 146.96 mph

Lotus — **1963** — Clark 127.74 mph

Ferrari — **1970** — Regazzoni 147.07 mph

1964 — **Ferrari** — Surtees 127.78 mph

1971 — **BRM** — Gethin 150.75 mph

BRM — **1965** — Stewart 130.46 mph

Lotus — **1972** — E. Fittipaldi 131.61 mph

1966 — **Ferrari** — Scarfiotti 135.93 mph

1973 — **Lotus** — Peterson 132.63 mph

Honda — **1967** — Surtees 140.50 mph

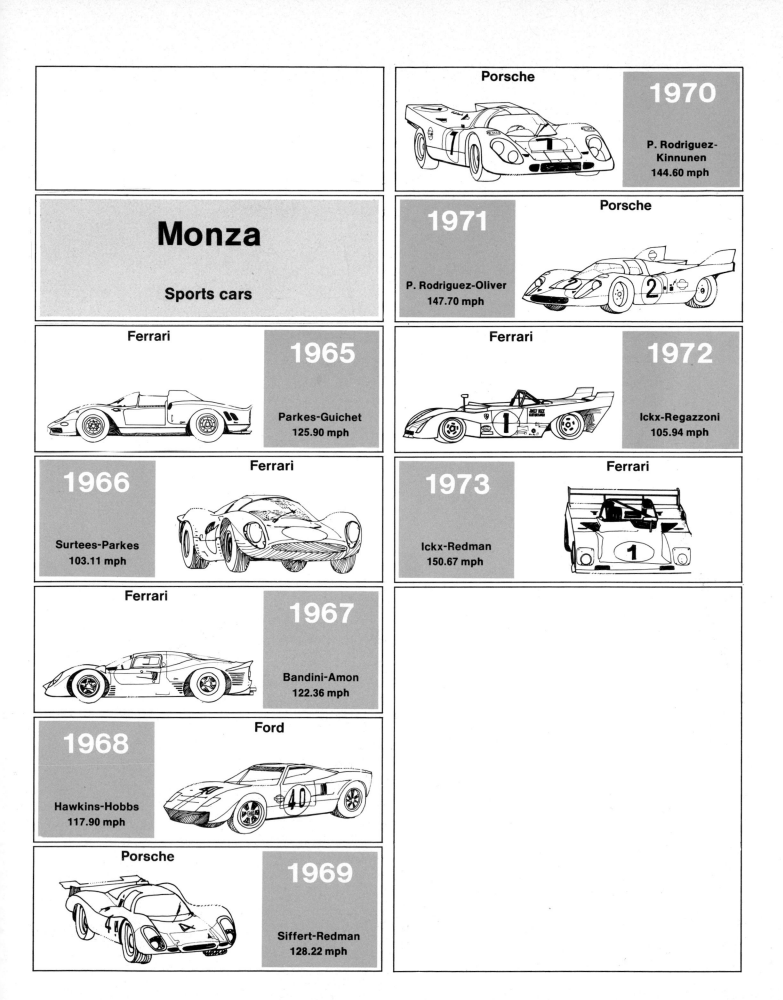

Monza

Sports cars

Porsche — **1970** — P. Rodriguez-Kinnunen — 144.60 mph

Porsche — **1971** — P. Rodriguez-Oliver — 147.70 mph

Ferrari — **1965** — Parkes-Guichet — 125.90 mph

Ferrari — **1972** — Ickx-Regazzoni — 105.94 mph

Ferrari — **1966** — Surtees-Parkes — 103.11 mph

Ferrari — **1973** — Ickx-Redman — 150.67 mph

Ferrari — **1967** — Bandini-Amon — 122.36 mph

Ford — **1968** — Hawkins-Hobbs — 117.90 mph

Porsche — **1969** — Siffert-Redman — 128.22 mph

Nürburgring

German Grand Prix

1935 Alfa Romeo

Nuvolari
75.16 mph

Mercedes **1927**

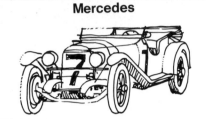

Merz
65.38 mph

1928 Mercedes

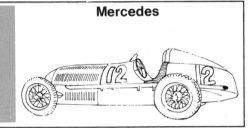

Caracciola-Werner
64.56 mph

Auto Union **1936**

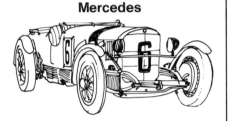

Rosemeyer
81.80 mph

Bugatti **1929**

Chiron
66.42 mph

1937 Mercedes

Caracciola
82.77 mph

1931 Mercedes

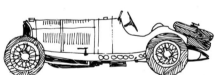

Caracciola
67.29 mph

Mercedes **1938**

Seaman
80.71 mph

Alfa Romeo **1932**

Caracciola
74.24 mph

1939 Mercedes

Caracciola
75.31 mph

1934 Auto Union

Stuck
76.37 mph

Ferrari **1950**

Alberto Ascari
77.67 mph

1951 Ferrari

Alberto Ascari
83.71 mph

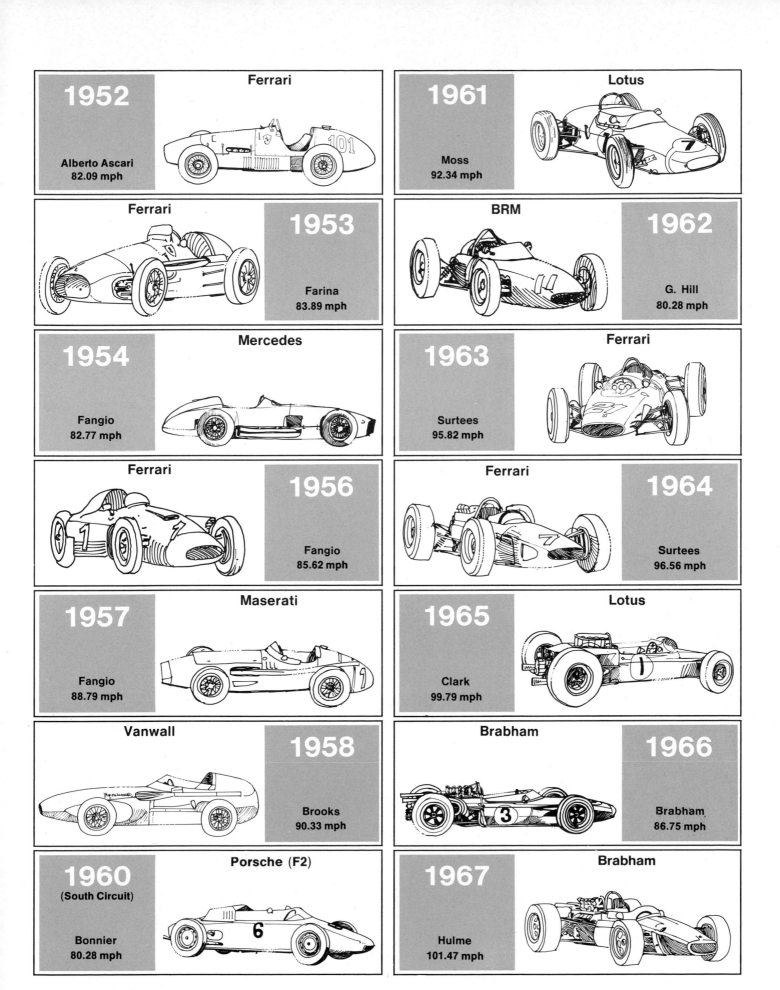

1952 Ferrari
Alberto Ascari
82.09 mph

Ferrari **1953**
Farina
83.89 mph

1954 Mercedes
Fangio
82.77 mph

Ferrari **1956**
Fangio
85.62 mph

1957 Maserati
Fangio
88.79 mph

Vanwall **1958**
Brooks
90.33 mph

1960
(South Circuit)
Bonnier
80.28 mph
Porsche (F2)

1961 Lotus
Moss
92.34 mph

BRM **1962**
G. Hill
80.28 mph

1963 Ferrari
Surtees
95.82 mph

Ferrari **1964**
Surtees
96.56 mph

1965 Lotus
Clark
99.79 mph

Brabham **1966**
Brabham
86.75 mph

1967 Brabham
Hulme
101.47 mph

1968

Matra

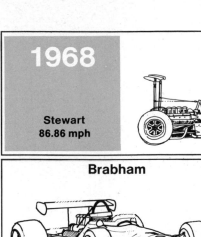

Stewart
86.86 mph

Brabham

1969

Ickx
108.43 mph

Nürburgring

Sports cars

1971

Tyrrell

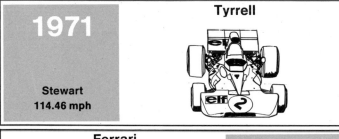

Stewart
114.46 mph

1953

Ferrari

Alberto Ascari-Farina
74.75 mph

Ferrari

1972

Ickx
116.63 mph

Maserati

1955

Behra
75.11 mph

1973

Tyrrell

Stewart
116.82 mph

1956

Maserati

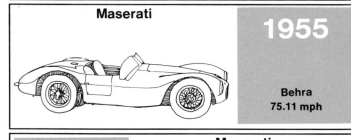

Moss-Behra-Taruffi-
Schell
80.59 mph

Aston Martin

1957

Brooks-
Cunningham-Reid
82.39 mph

1958

Aston Martin

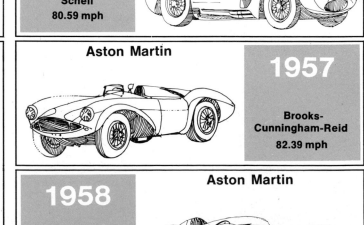

Moss-Brabham
84.26 mph

1959 **Aston Martin** Moss-Fairman 82.52 mph	**1966** **Chaparral** P. Hill-Bonnier 89.35 mph
Maserati **1960** Moss-Gurney 82.77 mph	**Porsche** **1967** Schutz-Buzzetta 90.40 mph
1961 **Maserati** Gregory-Cassner 79.10 mph	**1968** **Porsche** Siffert-Elford 94.80 mph
Ferrari **1962** P. Hill-Gendebien 82.39 mph	**Porsche** **1969** Siffert-Redman 100.97 mph
1963 **Ferrari** Surtees-Mairesse 82.72 mph	**1970** **Porsche** Elford-Ahrens 102.53 mph
Ferrari **1964** Scarfiotti-Vaccarella 86.90 mph	**Porsche** **1971** Elford-Larrousse 110.86 mph
1965 **Ferrari** Surtees-Scarfiotti 90.66 mph	**1972** **Ferrari** Peterson-Schenken 103.59 mph

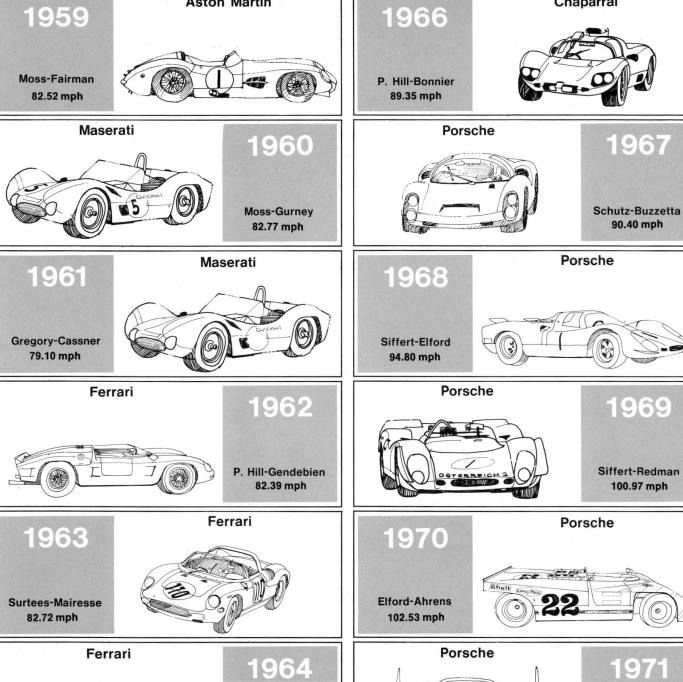
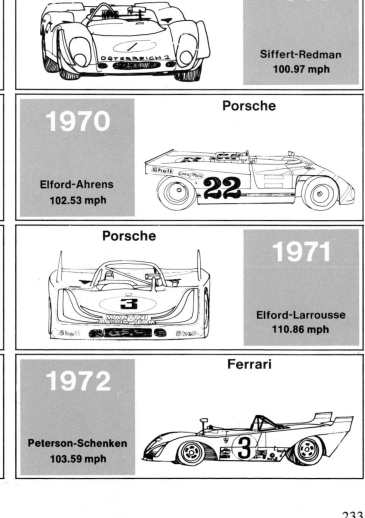
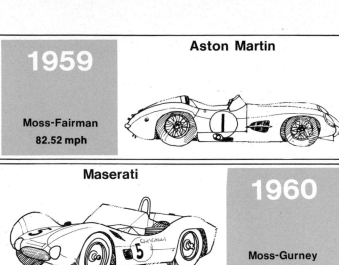
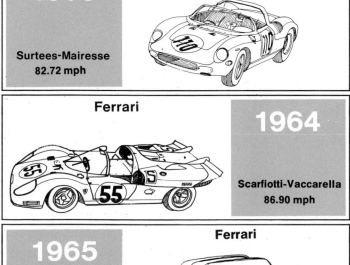

Ferrari

1973

Ickx-Redman
109.19 mph

Bugatti

1931

Williams-Conelli
82.01 mph

Maserati

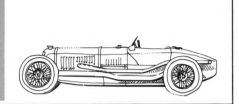

1933

Nuvolari
89.23 mph

Bugatti

1934

Dreyfus
86.91 mph

Mercedes

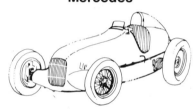

1935

Caracciola
97.87 mph

Spa-Francorchamps

Belgian Grand Prix

Auto Union

1937

Hasse
104.07 mph

Alfa Romeo

1925

Antonio Ascari
74.56 mph

Mercedes

1939

Lang
94.39 mph

Bugatti

1930

Chiron
72.10 mph

Alfa Romeo

1947

Wimille
95.28 mph

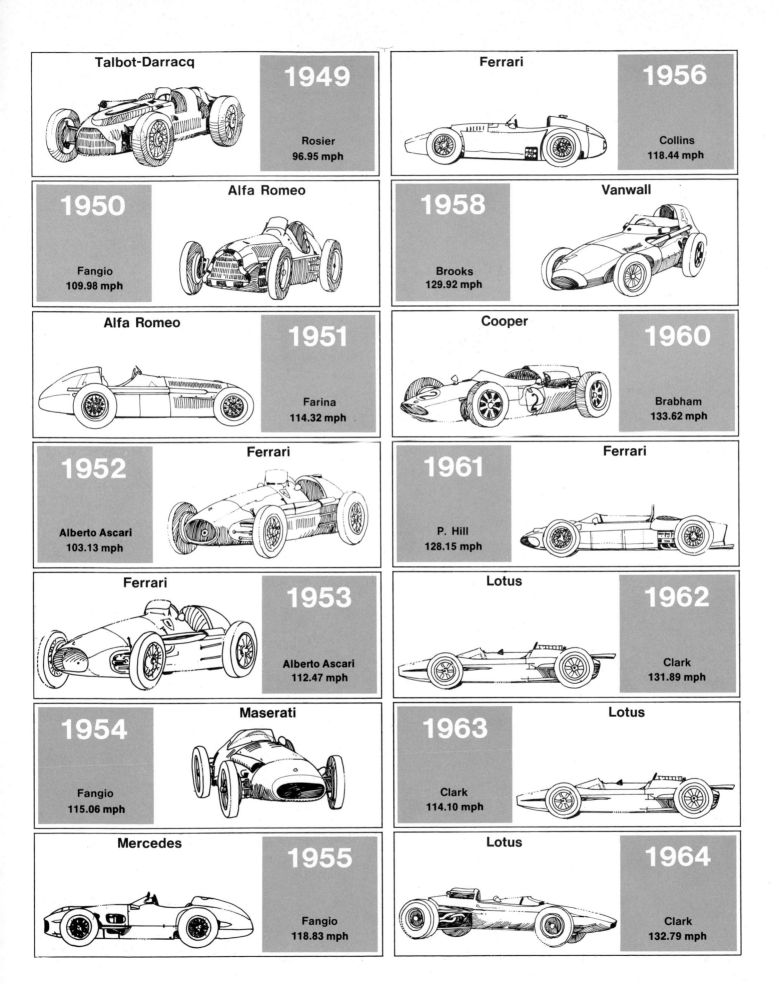

Talbot-Darracq — **1949** — Rosier — 96.95 mph

Alfa Romeo — **1950** — Fangio — 109.98 mph

Alfa Romeo — **1951** — Farina — 114.32 mph

Ferrari — **1952** — Alberto Ascari — 103.13 mph

Ferrari — **1953** — Alberto Ascari — 112.47 mph

Maserati — **1954** — Fangio — 115.06 mph

Mercedes — **1955** — Fangio — 118.83 mph

Ferrari — **1956** — Collins — 118.44 mph

Vanwall — **1958** — Brooks — 129.92 mph

Cooper — **1960** — Brabham — 133.62 mph

Ferrari — **1961** — P. Hill — 128.15 mph

Lotus — **1962** — Clark — 131.89 mph

Lotus — **1963** — Clark — 114.10 mph

Lotus — **1964** — Clark — 132.79 mph

Lotus

1965

Clark
117.16 mph

Ferrari

1966

Surtees
113.39 mph

Eagle

1967

Gurney
145.74 mph

McLaren

1968

McLaren
147.14 mph

BRM

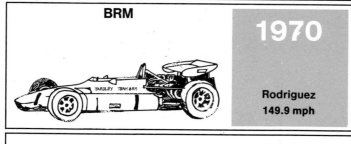

1970

Rodriguez
149.9 mph

Spa-Francorchamps

Sports cars

Lister Jaguar

1958

Gregory
121.23 mph

Porsche

1959

De Beaufort
110.80 mph

Porsche

1960

Frère
97.45 mph

Ferrari

1961

Mairesse
121.00 mph

Ferrari

1962
Berney
108.74 mph

Ferrari
1963

Mairesse
119.26 mph

Ferrari

1964
Parkes
124.40 mph

Ferrari
1965

Mairesse
125.74 mph

Ferrari

1966
Parkes-Scarfiotti
131.69 mph

Mirage
1967

Ickx-Thompson
120.48 mph

Ford

1968
Ickx-Redman
121.80 mph

Porsche

1969
Siffert-Redman
141.20 mph

Porsche
1970

Siffert-Redman
149.42 mph

Porsche

1971
P. Rodriguez-Oliver
154.77 mph

Ferrari
1972

Redman-Merzario
145.05 mph

Gulf-Mirage
1973

Bell-Hailwood
151.88 mph

Watkins Glen

U.S. Grand Prix

Lotus

1967

Clark
120.95 mph

Lotus

1961

Ireland
103.17 mph

Matra

1968

Stewart
124.89 mph

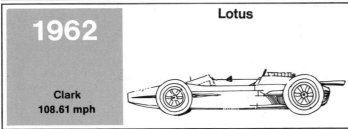

1962

Lotus

Clark
108.61 mph

Lotus

1969

Rindt
126.36 mph

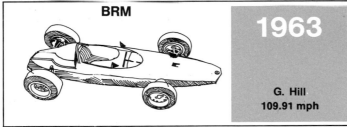

BRM

1963

G. Hill
109.91 mph

Lotus

1970

E. Fittipaldi
126.79 mph

1964

BRM

G. Hill
111.10 mph

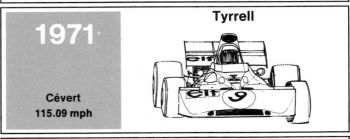

Tyrrell

1971

Cévert
115.09 mph

BRM

1965

G. Hill
107.98 mph

Tyrrell

1972

Stewart
117.48 mph

1966

Lotus

Clark
114.94 mph

JPS (Lotus)

1973

Peterson
118.05 mph

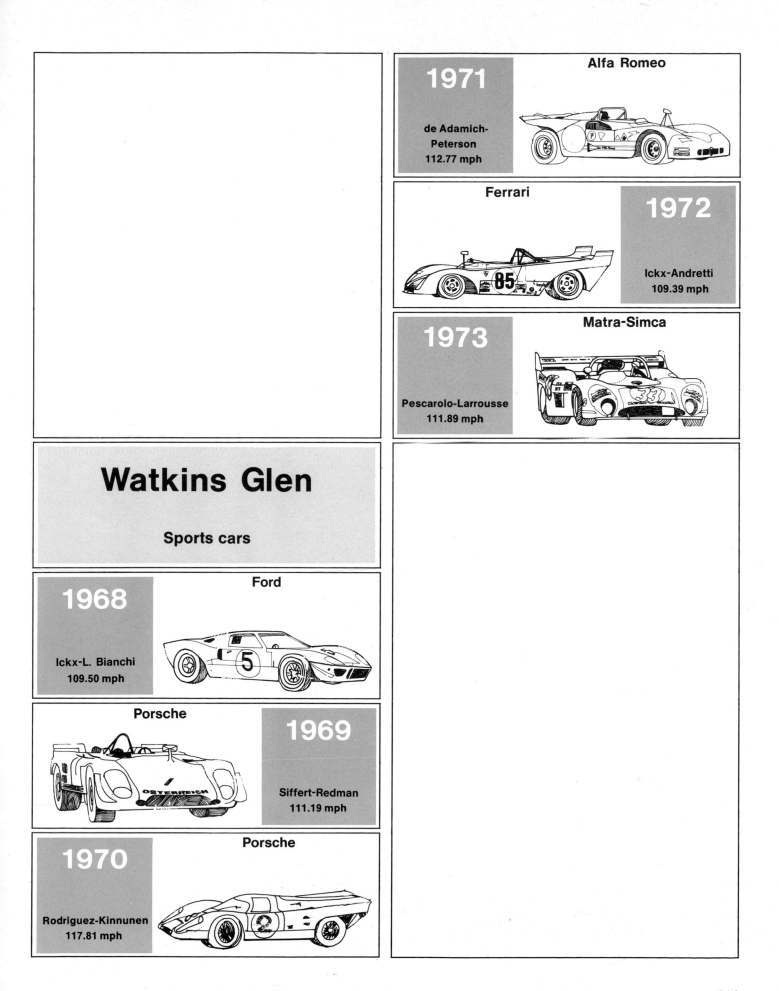

1971

Alfa Romeo

de Adamich-
Peterson
112.77 mph

Ferrari

1972

Ickx-Andretti
109.39 mph

1973

Matra-Simca

Pescarolo-Larrousse
111.89 mph

Watkins Glen

Sports cars

1968

Ford

Ickx-L. Bianchi
109.50 mph

Porsche

1969

Siffert-Redman
111.19 mph

1970

Porsche

Rodriguez-Kinnunen
117.81 mph